TIPS FOR SOCIAL STUDIES TEACHERS:/
ACTIVITIES FROM ERIC

Edited by Laurel R. Singleton

Social Science Education Consortium, Inc.
ERIC Clearinghouse for Social Studies/Social Science Education
Boulder, Colorado
1983

ORDERING INFORMATION

This publication is available from:

Social Science Education Consortium, Inc.
855 Broadway
Boulder, Colorado 80302

ISBN-0-89994-280-6

This publication was prepared with funding from the National Institute of Education, U.S. Department of Education, under contract no. 400-78-0006. The opinions expressed do not necessarily reflect the positions or policies of NIE or ED.

CONTENTS

PREFACE v

ACKNOWLEDGMENTS vi

INTRODUCTION 1

SECTION 1: DEVELOPING SOCIAL STUDIES SKILLS 7

    Surprise Appearance 9

    Message Relay 11

    K-Power 13

    Tasty Time Line 15

    Taste Test 23

    Newspaper Sleuths 27

SECTION 2: UNDERSTANDING MYSELF AND OTHERS 31

    Footprints 33

    Siblings 35

    Space Tower 37

    Cover-Up Game 43

    Families in the World of Make Believe 45

    In-Sight Game 47

SECTION 3: UNDERSTANDING CITIZENSHIP 51

    Why Rules? 53

    The Chowchilla Kidnapping Revisited 57

    The Candy Game 67

    It's Against the Law 69

    Legal Confusion 73

SECTION 4: UNDERSTANDING GEOGRAPHY 79

    Making Mountains 81

    The "Me" Map 83

    Map Quarters 85

    Be a Geographer 87

    No Place to Play 89

    The Flume 97

SECTION 5: UNDERSTANDING HISTORY 101

    There's an Old Trunk in My Attic 103

    My Folks Came in a Covered Wagon 109

    Should Men Have the Vote? 117

    What Would You Pack? 121

    The Land of Milk and Honey 131

SECTION 6: UNDERSTANDING THE WORLD 149

    The Pebble in the Pond 151

    Global Connections 157

    Match a Proverb and Find Its Home 161

    Human Rights 165

    World Food Supply 169

    Grab the Bananas 171

REFERENCES 175

PREFACE

In 1967, the ERIC system's mission was expanded from coverage of educational research to include coverage of education resources and practitioner-oriented materials as well. Despite the system's 15-year history in working with practice-related materials, some in the field still see the system as heavily weighted toward research. The recent ERIC Cost and Usage study indicated that the three most frequent uses of ERIC information are for research, for school improvement, and to support academic study.

Yet our experience at ERIC/ChESS clearly indicates that ERIC contains much material that can support classroom practice. For a number of years, the documents that we have submitted to the ERIC data base have been approximately half research-related materials and half materials oriented to practitioners and decision makers.

To bridge the apparent communication gap between ERIC and the field, we have prepared this volume of teaching activities drawn primarily from the ERIC system. We hope that users will find the activities not only useful, but a stimulant to investigate further the many teaching resources available through the ERIC system.

James E. Davis

Associate Director, ERIC Clearing-
    house for Social Studies/Social
    Science Education

Associate Director, Social Science
    Education Consortium, Inc.

ACKNOWLEDGMENTS

We would like to express our appreciation to the following organizations and individuals, who allowed us to reprint their materials in this publication:

--Albemarle County and Charlottesville City (Virginia) Public Schools

--Ms. Sarah M. Butzin, Florida State University

--Chelmsford (Massachusetts) Public Schools

--Center for Teaching International Relations

--ERA Press

--Global Perspectives in Education

--Dr. John D. Hoge, Boise State University

--Instructor Publications, Inc.

--Los Angeles Unified School District

--Dr. Wayne Mahood, State University College, Geneseo, New York

--Missouri Bar Association

--National Council on Geographic Education

--National Council for the Social Studies

--New Mexico Law-Related Education Project

--Ohio Bar Association

--Dr. Randall A. Pelow, Shippensburg (Pennsylvania) State College

--Research for Better Schools

--Dr. Dorothy Skeel, Peabody Center for Social Studies and Economic Education, Vanderbilt University

--Stauffer Communications, Inc.

--Dr. Ronald E. Sterling, University of Cincinnati

--Vermont State Department of Education

Special thanks is also due Sally Groft, whose skillful typing makes my job much easier.

Laurel R. Singleton

INTRODUCTION

Elementary and middle school social studies teachers are constantly looking for new teaching ideas to use in their classrooms. Their reasons may be varied: many may simply want to enliven their teaching and renew their own enthusiasm for the profession; others may feel a specific need for new, exciting activities to engage students caught up in the winter doldrums or spring fever. Time is often a factor--the time that teachers don't have to develop a great many new teaching activities themselves; the limited time that elementary teachers feel they can devote to social studies in face of demands to teach more reading, writing, and computation skills; and, for substitute teachers, the limited number of class periods they spend with the same students.

The ERIC system is one source of the practical ideas teachers seek. To illustrate that point, this book presents a range of social studies activities, most drawn from resources in the ERIC data base. The activities presented here are action-oriented, designed to stimulate student interest and participation while conveying important social studies content and skills. Most can be completed in one class period (although follow-up is always possible), so they can be used by substitutes who may not be in the same class the following day.

The activities are organized into six categories that cut across the areas typically covered in the elementary and middle school curriculum. The first section focuses on developing social studies skills, an essential part of every social studies program. The following five sections aim to develop student understanding of themselves and others as human beings, citizenship, geography, U.S. history, and global concerns. The activities within sections are not sequenced and do not depend on previous activities, although many could in fact be combined to advantage.

Some of the activities do require special materials or advance preparation. Often, however, the materials can be used over and over, so a cache of supplies set aside for these activities would allow use on short notice.

The chart on pages 2-5 provides an overview of all the activities, indicating grade level, topic or skill covered, preparation required, and special features.

Activity	Grade Level	Topic/ Skill	Preparation*	Special Features
Section 1: DEVELOPING SOCIAL STUDIES SKILLS				
Surprise Appearance	K-6	Observation skills	Gather materials; arrange for another staff member to visit your class (20 minutes)	Demonstration; large-group discussion
Message Relay	3-8	Communication skills	None	Demonstration; requires 5 students to be in hall for part of the class period
K-Power	3-8	Questioning and listening skills	Write rules on board; arrange desks into rows (5 minutes)	Game format adaptable to any content area
Tasty Time Line	1-3	Using a time line	Gather materials; copy data and picture cards (20 minutes)	Class constructs time line of "food facts"
Taste Test	4-6	Decision-making skills; consumer skills	Gather materials; copy handout (1 hour, including trip to grocery story)	Demonstration; requires students to eat a small amount of fruit in class
Newspaper Sleuths	5-8	Cooperative group work; parts of the newspaper	Collect several days' newspapers and divide into sections; prepare list of items to be found and write on chalkboard (30 minutes)	Small-group activity; scavenger hunt format adaptable to any content area
Section 2: UNDERSTANDING MYSELF AND OTHERS				
Footprints	K-3	How people are alike and different; graphing skills	Gather materials; draw axes for graphs on board (15 minutes)	Requires students to make tempera footprints; access to washing facilities needed
Siblings	5-8	Birth order; getting along with siblings	None	Small-group activity; some emotional reactions may be elicited
Space Tower	6-8	Group problem solving	Gather materials; copy handout (20 minutes)	Small-group activity; may be somewhat noisy; requires floor space

*Black-line masters and cards to be copied are provided with the activities. Other materials to be gathered are listed on the first page of each activity.

Activity	Grade Level	Topic/Skill	Preparation	Special Features
Cover-Up Game	2-8	Diversity; judging things by their appearance	Prepare pictures (30 minutes)	Also develops skills of visual interpretation
Families in the World of Make Believe	K-6	Stereotypes of families in children's literature	Obtain copies of fairy tales (15 minutes)	Small-group activity; some emotional reactions may be elicited
In-Sight Game	5-8	Sex equity	Prepare game materials (1½ hours)	Requires large playing area; may generate noise and controversy among students; game format adaptable to any content area

Section 3: UNDERSTANDING CITIZENSHIP

Activity	Grade Level	Topic/Skill	Preparation	Special Features
Why Rules?	K-4	Need for rules	Gather materials (20 minutes)	Game format; may be noisy
The Chowchilla Kidnapping Revisited	5-8	Need for rules based on societal values	Copy handouts (5 minutes)	Small-group discussion followed by large-group decision making
The Candy Game	1-6	Fairness of rules; how rules are made	Gather materials (30 minutes, including trip to store)	Game format; group discussion
It's Against the Law	4-8	Laws develop in response to changing needs	Copy handout (5 minutes)	Small-group activity; quick and easy
Legal Confusion	5-8	Clear and unclear laws	Copy handouts (5 minutes)	Worksheet and group discussion; quick and easy

Section 4: UNDERSTANDING GEOGRAPHY

Activity	Grade Level	Topic/Skill	Preparation	Special Features
Making Mountains	K-1	Landforms and bodies of water; models	Gather materials (1 hour)	Creating models; requires more than one class period
The "Me" Map	K-2	Maps; symbols	Gather materials (20 minutes)	Students map themselves; quick and easy

Activity	Grade Level	Topic/ Skill	Preparation	Special Features
Map Quarters	2-4	Symbols; scale	Gather materials (20 minutes)	Mapping; quick and easy
Be a Geographer	4-8	Mapping relative location; navigation	Rearrange classroom and gather materials (35 minutes)	Mapping activity; requires students to spend considerable time in the hall
No Place to Play	5-8	Land use	Copy handout and become familiar with case study (20 minutes)	Case study; simulated decision making; can be completed in one class period but probably more effective if extended
The Flume	4-6	Energy	Make flumes and question cards (1 hour)	Game format and learning device adaptable to any content area

Section 5: UNDERSTANDING HISTORY

Activity	Grade Level	Topic/ Skill	Preparation	Special Features
There's an Old Trunk in My Attic	1-3	Historical sense; writing skills	Gather materials (1-2 hours)	Requires more than one class period
My Folks Came in a Covered Wagon	4-6	Children's lives on the American frontier	Copy handout (5 minutes)	Small-group analysis of primary source material; quick and easy
Should Men Have the Vote?	7-8	Suffrage; sex stereotyping	Copy handout (5 minutes)	May generate controversy
What Would You Pack?	5-8	Immigration	Copy handouts (10 minutes)	Small-group card-sort activity; quick and easy
The Land of Milk and Honey	7-8	Immigration quotas	Copy handouts; gather materials (45 minutes, including trip to grocery store)	Simulation; brief but effective

Section 6: UNDERSTANDING THE WORLD

Activity	Grade Level	Topic/ Skill	Preparation	Special Features
The Pebble in the Pond	1-4	Cause and effect	Copy handout; gather materials (45 minutes)	Demonstration
Global Connections	3-8	Relationship of class members to other nations	Copy handouts (10 minutes)	Game format; quick and easy--perhaps somewhat noisy

Activity	Grade Level	Topic/Skill	Preparation	Special Features
Match a Proverb and Find Its Home	5-8	Folk wisdom	None	Game format; quick and easy
Human Rights	5-8	Declaration of children's rights	Copy handout (10 minutes)	Small-group decision making; gives students power
World Food Supply	3-6	Maldistribution of resources	Gather materials (30 minutes, including trip to store)	Simple simulation
Grab the Bananas	6-8	Conflict resolution	Draw matrix on board (5 minutes)	Simulation; quick and easy to implement; requires good debriefing

Many of the activities were drawn from teacher-developed units or guides that contain other activities that would be of interest to teachers. The source of each activity is given on the first page of the activity description. Directions for ordering sources from ERIC and/or the original publisher and a brief annotation for each source document are presented in the reference list at the end of the book.

If you have developed a social studies unit or series of activities that you would like to make available to other practitioners, submit two copies of your document to Acquisitions, ERIC/ChESS, 855 Broadway, Boulder, CO 80302. Your document will be evaluated by the ERIC/ChESS staff on the basis of such criteria as reproducibility and quality. If your document is selected for entry into the ERIC data base, it will be announced to the 5000 organizations that receive Resources in Education, be made available on microfiche to the 700 libraries having the ERIC collection, and will always be in print. Thus, you can contribute to helping the ERIC system remain responsive to the needs of social studies teachers!

Section 1
DEVELOPING SOCIAL STUDIES SKILLS

The skills falling under the aegis of social studies are many and varied. The six activities in this section reflect that diversity, targeting a number of skills for development. The first activity, "Surprise Appearance," aims to help students develop observation skills. The next two activities, "Message Relay" and "K-Power," both focus on communication skills. As its title implies, "Tasty Time Line" introduces students to the use of time lines in historical analysis. "Taste Test" helps students improve their decision-making skills, using consumer decisions as a case study. The final activity, "Newspaper Sleuths," targets the skills of cooperative group work for development; this activity also introduces students to the parts of the newspaper.

SURPRISE APPEARANCE

Overview

One way in which children's ability to use direct observation is evidenced is by a growing capacity to use all of their senses. A second indication of this ability is a growing capacity to make good and rational decisions about which senses to trust on given occasions. Thus, children need the opportunity to build the capacity to use all their senses and to evaluate the strengths and limitations of each. This activity is designed to provide such an opportunity.

Objectives: At the conclusion of this activity, students will be better able to:

--observe and report data from a personal experience

--identify settings or situations in which their ears are especially helpful, occasions when their noses supply important information, etc.

Grade Level: K-6

Materials and Preparation: Plan for a member of the school staff to make a quick surprise visit to your class. He/she should be dressed in an unusual fashion and perhaps be carrying some rather unusual object. You will also need some salt or sugar, a realistic looking piece of plastic fruit, a glass of fruit-flavored drink or colored water, and a liquid having a strong aroma (perfume or kerosene).

Procedure

1. Open the activity with the prearranged "surprise appearance" by a staff member. After the visit, ask the class to describe--in detail--the person who came in. Ask such questions as: What was the

---

Adapted from Teacher's Guide to the Basic Competencies in Reasoning (Vermont State Department of Education, 1978), p. 3; and Skill Development in Elementary Social Studies: A New Perspective, by Barbara J. Winston and Charlotte C. Anderson (Social Science Education Consortium and ERIC Clearinghouse for Social Studies/Social Science Education, 1977), pp. 8-10. Used by permission.

9

person wearing? What was being carried? What did the person do while in the classroom? Was the person wearing glasses? Was the person wearing perfume or cologne? Did the person speak loudly or softly?

2. Compare student responses with a full description of the visitor prepared in advance. Ask students to speculate about reasons for the differences. Ask: How did we gather our information about the visitor? Which senses gave us the most information? The least?

3. Display the salt or sugar, plastic fruit, glass of fruit-flavored drink or colored water, and aromatic liquid. Ask students how they could best learn about these objects. What is the white powder? How could children identify it? Is the fruit real? How can the children tell? What is the liquid in the glass? How could children identify it? What is the second liquid? How could children identify it? Emphasize that while we can indeed learn a great deal through the sense of taste, tasting unidentified substances can be very dangerous. We should not taste something unless we know it is safe to do so. Our other senses can sometimes help us decide.

4. Tell students to imagine that they are outdoors on a cold, clear, windy day. Which sense organs or sensory impressions would help them know that the sun was shining? (Eyes, sense of warmth on the skin). Which senses would tell them if the wind were blowing? (They could see tree branches swaying, hear the rustle of wind, feel air moving). Discuss what other information they could gather through their five senses.

Follow-up

A "sense walk" can provide a good lesson in observing. Instruct children to gather information with only one sense or with one sense blocked (e.g., wearing a blindfold, with cotton in their ears, with gloves on their hands). Later, give them the opportunity to reflect on their experiences and discuss them with others. Places to take children for "sense walks" might include the school gym, both during a class and when one is not in session; the lunchroom and kitchen while meals are being prepared; an open setting, such as a forest preserve, during different seasons; a business district early in the morning and at midday.

MESSAGE RELAY

Overview

In this variation of the old "telephone" game, students are provided with the opportunity to observe how messages are changed when they are communicated from one person to another. A follow-up discussion helps students analyze the types of errors that are introduced in verbal communication.

Objectives: At the conclusion of this activity, students will be better able to:

--identify factors that affect the accuracy of communications

--accurately pass on a report containing an account of an event

Grade Level: 3-8

Materials and Preparation: Students will need pencils and paper.

Procedure

1. Select a team of five students and ask them to step outside the room for a few minutes. Ask them to quietly discuss a social studies topic the class has been covering while they wait to be called back to class.

2. Have the rest of the class devise a brief report about the same topic. Students should jot down the report so that they will be better able to tell where and when changes are introduced.

3. Call the first team member back into the room. Ask one class member to read the report to the first team member.

Adapted from Interdependence and Social Interaction: Our Human Ties, Monograph #4, by Maxine R. Mitchell and others (Los Angeles Unified School District, copyright 1976), p. 16. Permission to reprint granted by the Los Angeles Unified School District. Follow-up ideas from Social Studies for the Visually Impaired Child, by Laurel R. Singleton (Social Science Education Consortium, 1980). Used by permission.

4. Ask this team member to tell the report to the next team member, keeping it as nearly identical to the original report as possible. Repeat this process until all five members of the team have received the report. Class members should listen carefully to the relaying of the report, noting any changes from the original.

5. Ask students to compare each report with the original and to identify at what points alterations occurred.

6. Discuss the factors which affected the accuracy of the communication process (e.g., word substitution, omission of parts, addition of parts, rapid speech, indistinct speech, inattentive listening). Discuss how these problems could be avoided.

Follow-up

A wide range of activities can be used to develop students' listening skills, a vital part of the process of communicating. Younger students can profit from such activities as listening to and identifying a variety of environmental sounds (either heard in the classroom or tape-recorded), playing simple games that involve careful listening (e.g., "Simon Says"), or retelling simple stories that have been read aloud by the teacher. Older students can benefit from opportunities for structured listening. Follow the playing of a tape or the reading of a story with questions that test comprehension. Before reading material aloud, give students a list of questions whose answers they should listen for. Tailor the questions asked to the needs of your class; for example, for a group of sixth-graders who are having difficulty interpreting oral information, the questions might require students to identify the main idea of a passage, predict outcomes, and paraphrase. Students can also work in pairs, with one student explaining his or her views on a particular topic followed by the other student's rephrasing of those views in a way that demonstrates understanding and is acceptable to the original speaker. The two can then change roles and repeat the process.

Overview

This game has several purposes. First, it builds questioning and listening skills while reviewing content. It also aims to increase the value that students place on having knowledge by modeling the reality that knowledge is power. It also provides a means of assessing students' knowledge. The game requires that students listen to one another, allowing time for their classmates to formulate questions and think about answers. Thus, it is not necessarily fast-paced. It is effective, however, in involving students of all ability levels.

Objectives: At the conclusion of this activity, students will be better able to:

--frame questions related to social studies content

--answer questions related to social studies content

Grade Level: 3-8

Materials and Preparation: The game will be most effective if some type of reward/reinforcement points are available. Select several categories about which students can ask questions; write these categories on the chalkboard. Also write the following rules:

--If you ask a question, you must be able to answer it.

--Questions must relate to the categories on the chalkboard.

--Questions must have at least one right answer.

--Questions must be original; do not take a question from a textbook or worksheet.

--You must be able to remember the question and its answer without writing them down.

--No riddles or trick questions.

--No questions with long, multiple-part answers.

If your class is not arranged in rows, organize the desks into rows.

Activity by John D. Hoge, Boise State University. Used by permission.

Procedure

1. Explain to students that they are going to play a game called K-POWER. K stands for knowledge. The object of the game is for students to move to the front of the room and stay there by asking questions and using their K-POWER. Each time you play the game, have different students start at the front of the rows.

2. Explain that the first person in each row will ask a question related to one of the categories on the chalkboard. Example categories and their point values might be: social studies (5 points), science (4 points), and math (3 points); or Revolutionary War (5 points), American Indians (5 points), and early presidents (5 points). The student in the first seat of the first row begins the game by picking a category and posing a question related to it to classmates in the same row. If the teacher judges the question to be in violation of the rules, the questioner has one chance to reformulate it. If the teacher judges the question to be fair, the last student in the row attempts to answer it or passes the chance to the next student in the row. The first student to answer the question correctly receives the point award and exchanges seats with the questioner.

3. If none of the students in the row can answer a question, the question becomes fair game for anyone in another row. If a student in another row answer the question correctly, he or she exchanges seats with the questioner. (Limit the number of guesses from the other rows; allowing unlimited guesses slows down the game and makes it almost impossible to ask a question that cannot be answered.)

4. If the question cannot be answered, the questioner receives the point award, remains in the first seat, and gets to ask another question when play returns to her or his row.

5. Play then passes to the next row, which repeats the process. Never play the game longer than it holds students' interest.

Follow-up

As a variation, introduce students to levels of questions, increasing the reward for higher-level questions.

TASTY TIME LINE

Overview

Young children often experience difficulty understanding time beyond yesterday, today, and tomorrow. Placing events in a historical framework can thus be a tall order for many youngsters. This activity helps students promote the organization of information and history through a time line on a topic of immediate interest--the history of such popular foods as pizza and hot dogs. Many primary-grade children who are turned off by written reports find this an appealing option.

Objectives: At the conclusion of this activity, students will be better able to:

--use a time line to organize historical information

Grade Level: 1-3

Materials and Preparation: You will need a copy of the data and picture cards. Depending on the time available, you may want to collect additional relevant facts in advance through such sources as almanacs, encyclopedias, and trivia books, or assign a small group of children to research such facts. Prepare, or have the children prepare, data and picture cards to illustrate the additional facts. You will also need white shelving paper, colored cellophane tape, colored gummed disks, and felt-tip pens.

Procedure

1. Launch the lesson by asking students: Have you ever wondered when someone ate the first slice of pizza? When an ice cream cone was first served? Explain that foods such as these haven't always been around and ask if students would like to know when and where they

Adapted from "A Tasty Time Line," by Cloe Giampaolo, in "Basic Curriculum," Teacher 97, no. 5 (February 1980), pp. 82-83. Copyright 1980, Macmillan Professional Magazines. Used by permission of The Instructor Publications, Inc.

first appeared. Explain that you know a way to arrange this kind of information.

2. Have students brainstorm a list of their favorite foods. Popular choices are pizza, ice cream cones, potato chips, chewing gum, soda, and candy bars.

3. Write "time line" on the board and ask a volunteer to draw a picture of what "line" means on the board. Ask students to help you list units of time. Ask: Which unit would make the most sense on a time line that covers a lot of long-ago events? Day? Month? Year? If students don't understand that year is the best choice, point out that you will be covering about 300 years of time.

4. Once students understand the idea of a time line, relate the facts about favorite foods provided on the data cards. Emphasize dates so that the students begin to digest the idea of "long, long ago," "not too long ago," and "recently."

5. Direct students in constructing a bulletin-board display of the time line. Mount the shelving paper on the bulletin board and stick on the tape as the baseline. Explain that you will start with the year 1700 on the end of the baseline and add the gummed disks at 50-year intervals until you reach the year 2000. Give students plenty of time to absorb the intervals. As you write each date below the time line, call on a student to paste a colored disk above that date directly on the line. Measure and section off each date evenly and display the picture cards along the bulletin-board ledge.

6. Place the data cards face down in a pile and ask volunteers to select cards. Each child reads aloud the information on the card (with your assistance if needed), matches it to its corresponding picture card, and locates its position on the time line. The child then tacks the drawing and information card above or below the date. Ask students to think carefully about the dates. Ask such questions as: Is 1886 closer to 1850 or 1900?

7. When you come to the year 2000, put a big question mark above the year with a card that says "What next?" Ask the students to speculate on future popular foods. Will we be eating "gravity pies," "satellite subs," and "space cones"?

8.   Finally, brainstorm a title for the time line, trace it in black letters, and pin it to the bulletin board.

Follow-up

Have students follow up on the discussion of foods of the future, drawing or writing a brief description of a meal in the year 2000. Encourage other students to construct their own time lines. They may want to depict events in their own lives; investigate a personal interest, such as sports or toys; or tackle something even more ambitious.

MIDDLE OF 1700s PIZZA FIRST SERVED IN ITALY	1853 POTATO CHIPS FIRST SERVED
1860 CHEWING GUM FIRST SOLD IN STORES	1890 FIRST HOT DOG SOLD
1904 ICE CREAM CONE INVENTED	1921 "BABY RUTH" CANDY BAR FIRST SOLD
EARLY 1950s POPCORN FIRST SOLD IN PACKAGES	1968 "BIG MAC" BORN

TASTE TEST

Overview

This activity focuses on decision-making skills applied in a consumer context. Students conduct a taste test of three brands of the same food product and then analyze the factors that go into a decision to purchase one of the brands.

Objectives: At the conclusion of this activity, students will be better able to:
--define the terms "brand name," "house brand," and "generic"
--discuss how personal values influence consumer choices

Grade Level: 4-6

Materials and Preparation: You will need copies of Handout 1 for all the students, as well as a can opener, toothpicks, and cans of pineapple chunks or other fruit available locally under three types of labels: national brand, house or store brand, and generic. Provide enough cans so that each student can sample one piece of fruit from each type of can. Cover the labels of the cans with aluminum foil or heavy paper, coding them Brand A, B, and C. Make sure all prices are removed or obscured. Open the cans and place them, along with the toothpicks, on a table in the front of the room.

Procedure

1. Distribute copies of Handout 1 and go over the directions. Ask students to sample one piece of each brand. Everyone should sample A first and then come back for B and then C. Allow students to discuss the qualities of each brand.

Adapted from Consumer Education Learning Activities, by Jerry Forkner and Gail Schatz (Social Science Education Consortium and ERIC Clearinghouse for Social Studies/Social Science Education, 1980), pp. 25-26. Used by permission. Follow-up idea from "Handle Holiday Havoc: Teach with Toys!," Keeping Up (December 1982), p. 3. Used by permission.

2. After students have tasted the three items and filled out the first part of the handout, discuss what differences between brands (color, size, etc.), if any, students tasted or observed.

3. Explain that one can of fruit is a store or house brand, one is a name brand, and one is generic. (If necessary, offer the following explanation: A house brand is a store's own brand. It is likely to be cheaper than a nationally advertised or name brand, such as Del Monte, because advertising costs are lower. Many housebrands are produced by the same companies that make name brands. A generic-label product has no brand name. The black-and-white label gives only product information. Since it is not advertised at all and has a plain label, it is likely to be the lowest priced. Generic products may not be uniform in taste, consistency, color, size, or other qualities; they are normally described as "suitable for everyday use.")

4. Poll the class as to which brand they prefer and why. Post the responses.

5. Uncover the labels and announce the price of each product. Then discuss the following questions:

--Could you guess the name brand, house brand, and generic brand by sight and taste alone? Why (or why not)?

--Would you change your decision about which brand you would buy now that you know the prices? Why (or why not)?

--Are the most expensive products always the best quality? How is "best" determined?

--Is an item a "good buy" just because it is cheap? Why (or why not)?

--Why do people buy brand-name products? Is there sometimes peer pressure to buy certain brands (for example, Levi's, Adidas)?

Follow-up

Further examine the impact of values on consumer decisions by having students compare holiday mail order catalogs from the past with those of today. What toys have been popular for many years? Why? What lasting values do they represent? What toys have come and gone? Why? Will today's most popular toys still be popular in 20 years?

PRODUCT EVALUATION FORM

<u>Directions</u>: You are going to conduct a "blind" test of three brands of
fruit. Rate each product on each characteristic listed below, using the
following scale: 1 = high quality, 2 = medium quality, 3 = low quality.

Item	Taste	Appearance	Texture	Price
A				
B				
C				

<u>Before price is known</u>: Which item would you buy? Why?

<u>After price is known</u>: Which item would you buy? Why?

NEWSPAPER SLEUTHS

Overview

This activity involves students in searching through the newspaper for particular items of information. To find all the information required, students must work cooperatively. Depending on the list of items to be found, this activity can be used to increase awareness of current events, reinforce such skills as differentiating between fact and opinion and interpreting political cartoons, encourage development of good consumer skills, or make students aware of prejudices reflected in media coverage of certain groups or areas.

Objectives: At the conclusion of this activity, students will be better able to:

--identify the parts of the newspaper

--use the skills of cooperative group work

--apply selected skills reflected in the teacher's choice of items to be found

Grade Level: 5-8

Materials and Preparation: You will need several newspapers divided into the various sections: news, editorial, sports, classified, features, etc. If you are using this activity in a consumer education unit, you may want to use Wednesday's and Sunday's papers, since those editions generally have the most advertisements. Before using the activity, prepare a list of items to be found, making sure that all parts of the paper must be used to complete the list. Write the list on the chalkboard. Some sample items are provided at the end of the activity.

This activity is based on an idea suggested in "More Miracle Motivators for Reluctant Readers," by Nicholas P. Criscuolo, Instructor 89, no. 8 (March 1980), p. 73. Copyright 1980 by The Instructor Publications, Inc. Used by permission.

Procedure

1.   Divide the class into groups of three or four students. Give each group one newspaper, instructing them to divide up the parts of the paper among the group members. Tell the students they will have 10 minutes to find the list of items on the chalkboard. (Set the time so that it is reasonable given the length of the list, but short enough so that students will need to do some cooperative planning; i.e., divide up the items that they are looking for according to the sections of the newspaper.)

2.   At the end of the 20-minute period, have students report on the items found, indicating in what section they were located and what conclusions they can draw from that location. Help students arrive at a general description of the contents of each section of the newspaper.

3.   Ask students who completed the entire list what strategies their group used that were helpful. Did they divide their list among the group members? Use skimming techniques? Ask groups what problems they had, and probe for suggestions on how they might have avoided or resolved the problems. Conclude the activity with a discussion of effective techniques for cooperative group work.

Sample Items

1.   Find a good buy on cat food.
2.   Find an editorial that deals with a local problem.
3.   Find the cheapest price for a 19-inch color television set.
4.   Find the latest news about a person you admire.
5.   Find an article about an important current event.
6.   Find an article about the most important event of the day.
7.   Find a factual article and an opinion article about the same topic.
8.   Find the sports score in which the two teams or competitors had the widest variation in their scores.
9.   Find one article about events in each of the continents.
10. Find a cartoon criticizing the president or another public figure.
11. Find a cartoon supporting the president or another public figure.
12. Find an article about a world leader who is a woman.
13. Find an article about a world leader who is over 70 years old.
14. Find an article about a world leader who is under 40 years old.
15. Find two articles about the same sport, one reporting on female athletes, the other on male athletes.

16. Find a picture of a local leader.
17. Find a column that provides advice.
18. Find an ad for a job that pays between $10.00 and $15.00 an hour.

Follow-up

Have the class create a bulletin board display on the parts of the newspaper. Assign one section of the newspaper to each group, instructing each to develop a definition or description of that section of the paper on which all group members can agree, print the definition on a piece of paper, and select clippings from the paper to illustrate the definition.

Section 2
UNDERSTANDING MYSELF AND OTHERS

The activities in this section are designed to develop student understanding of concepts that will help them in their efforts to get along with others. The first activity, "Footprints," is intended to teach early elementary students that while all people are different, they all have common needs and desires as well. The following two activities focus on getting along with others; "Siblings" provides students with opportunities to discuss their relationships with brothers and sisters, while "Space Tower" increases student awareness of effective group processes. The final three activities focus on different kinds of stereotyping. "Cover-Up Game" demonstrates the inappropriateness of judging things by their appearance. "Families in the World of Make Believe" highlights the stereotyping of different family styles that is pervasive in children's literature. The "In-Sight Game" requires students to work cooperatively while reviewing knowledge related to sex equity.

FOOTPRINTS

Overview

This activity opens with students' gathering and graphing data about shoe sizes and styles worn by class members. They then make and compare tempera footprints. A closing discussion helps students understand that while people share many commonalities, each person is also unique.

Objectives: At the conclusion of this activity, students will be better able to:

--collect and graph data about the characteristics of their classmates

--list ways in which all people are alike and different

Grade Level: K-3

Materials and Preparation: Before this activity, draw the axes for two graphs on the chalkboard; one should plot number of students against shoe size, while the other should plot number of students against shoe style. You will also need tempera spread on trays and butcher paper for this activity.

Procedure

1. Tell students that they are going to be studying their feet today. Have students brainstorm a list of all the things they could find out about feet. If they have trouble getting started, provide some initial suggestions (e.g., how many bones are in a human foot, how many miles a first-grader's feet walk in one day, etc.). Record students' suggestions on the chalkboard. If students do not mention shoe size and shoe style, point to the blank graphs on the chalkboard and suggest that these might be two areas that would be easy to study.

Adapted from Building Self Concept: Our Human Ties, Monograph #2 (Los Angeles Unified School District, copyright 1976), p. 36. Permission to reprint granted by the Los Angeles Unified School District.

2. Conduct a survey of shoe sizes worn by class members. Have students assist you in displaying this information on the graph on the chalkboard. Repeat the process for shoe styles, using such broad categories as tennis or running shoes, boots, loafers, and sandals. Use the graph to illustrate that many people have the same shoe size and choose the same shoe styles.

3. Ask: Many people have the same size shoe. Does that mean their feet are the same? How might their feet be different?

4. Have each child make a tempera footprint of the right foot on the butcher paper. You may want to have students group their footprints on the paper according to their shoe size. Allow students plenty of time to compare their footprints in some detail, noting differences in patterns of whorls and loops and in the number of lines per toe, etc.

5. Conclude the activity with a discussion of the fact that while people are alike in many ways, each person is also unique.

Follow-up

Have students use the footprints to create a bulletin board display. Have a contest to find the best title for the display. Allow interested students to research other information about feet suggested in the brainstorming session. Encourage them to present their findings to the class using graphs and charts.

SIBLINGS

Overview

One of the most persistent and continuing sources of confusion and often of conflict for young people is that of sibling relationships. Teachers can help young people understand and deal more effectively with siblinghood by setting up a format through which students can share perceptions and experiences with one another and thus gain insights into the problems and the possibilities for change.

Objectives: At the conclusion of this activity, students will be better able to:

--list some advantages and disadvantages associated with being the oldest, youngest, middle, or only child

--describe possible solutions to problems growing out of sibling relationships

Grade Level: 5-8

Materials and Preparation: No materials or preparation are needed.

Procedure

1. Divide the class into four groups: firstborns, middle children, youngest children, and only children. Have the groups meet separately for 10 minutes to plan a report to the class on the problems and advantages of their particular place in the family. The report should include a look at popular misconceptions that other groups might have. If students have difficulty starting their discussions, ask these questions: What is the worst thing about being oldest (youngest, etc.)? The best? Has anyone ever said "You're spoiled because you're an only child" or "Youngest children are always babyish?" How do you feel about these statements?

Adapted from Developing Human Potential: A Handbook of Activities for Personal and Social Growth, by Robert and Isabel Hawley (Education Research Associates, 1975), pp. 38, 41. Used by permission of Education Research Associates, Box 767-EC, Amherst, MA 01004.

2. Give each group five minutes to present its report, or convene a panel composed of four students, one from each group. If the panel format is used, give each panelist two or three minutes to state his or her group's position in regard to siblings, and then open the floor for questions.

3. Hold a general discussion, identifying those elements of sibling relationships or family life that seem unique to individuals, those that seem to be common to a particular group, and those that are common to the class as a whole. The discussion can then focus on what can be done to make sibling relationships more satisfactory.

Follow-up

Sibling relationships abound with opportunities for role playing. The teacher can take a concrete situation which has been raised in discussion and then, using role-reversal, ask one of the firstborns to play the role of the youngest and a youngest to play firstborn, etc. After a brief enactment (no more than four minutes), cut the role play short and ask the students (1) how it feels to be on the other side, and (2) how effective the strategies reflected in the role play might be for handling sibling relationships.

SPACE TOWER

Overview

This activity is designed to make students more aware of and able to use skills that support active collaboration in problem solving. These skills include the ability to appreciate and build on the efforts of others, the ability to give and receive useful feedback, the ability to listen actively and to empathize, the ability to both seek and give direction, the ability to trust others and elicit trust from others, and the ability to use group planning as a cooperative strengthening power rather than as a competitive, divisive force.

Objectives: At the conclusion of this activity, students will be better able to:

--list processes that facilitate solving a group problem

--demonstrate skills that are important in solving a group problem

--describe how competitiveness within a group interferes with group problem solving

Grade Level: 6-8

Materials and Preparation: You will need several copies of Handout 2. Because the role of the group process observer is so important, you may want to go over this handout with the class before the activity begins, explaining such terms as "individually directed positive feedback." You will also need used computer cards, scissors, and baseballs or old newspapers or magazines, masking tape, and books. Students will need paper and pencils.

Adapted from Developing Human Potential: A Handbook of Activities for Personal and Social Growth, by Robert and Isabel Hawley (Education Research Associates, 1975), pp. 56-59. Used by permission of Education Research Associates, Box 767-EC, Amherst, MA 01004.

Procedure

1. Divide the class into groups of six to eight students. One student should be the process observer and should receive a copy of Handout 2. The process observer sits outside the group and takes no part in their task. The observer's job is to see how the group is functioning and to identify any particular things that help or hinder its functioning.

2. Give each group a three-inch stack of computer cards, two pairs of scissors, and one baseball. Give the students the following instructions: You are to design and build a tower which will support the baseball as high from the floor as possible. No props such as walls or chairs may be used. You will be allowed ten minutes for planning and ten minutes for construction. During the planning period, you may touch the material and experiment with structures if you wish, but none of the material you touch during the planning period may go into the construction. In other words, no prefabrication will be allowed. (An alternative task would be to use newspapers or magazines and tape to construct a bridge that will support four textbooks and be high and wide enough for a box 12" by 16" to pass under.)

3. At the end of the planning period, ask the students to reflect on how satisfied they were with the process that the group used in planning. For later reference, each student should write down a number from one to seven to represent their degree of satisfaction, with one being very dissatisfied and seven very satisfied. Then ask the students to write down a second number, again from one to seven, to represent their satisfaction with the plan that the group has decided upon. These numbers can be put away for the discussion following the completion of the building.

4. Instruct the students to begin building. Announce the time remaining at the end of five, eight, and nine minutes.

5. Allow two or three minutes for the group members to examine the other groups' products. Then have the small groups reconvene and spend five minutes in a small-group discussion. The process observer should report first.

6. Each group should briefly report to the class on their findings, and the entire class should discuss issues of collaboration and competition, leadership, and procedures for making the process more effective and satisfactory for all.

Follow-up

This follow-up activity illustrates the effects of positive and negative feedback on group participation; the editor of this book vividly remembers its impact from a student council workshop attended more than 15 years ago! Divide the class into groups of six or seven students, explaining that they will be discussing a controversial topic encountered recently in their social studies classes (specify an appropriate topic) and trying to reach a group consensus on the topic. At the same time, they will be examining the effects of coming late on group work.

Ask two students in each group to volunteer to be the latecomers and one student to serve as an observer. Send the latecomers out of the classroom. Then explain to the groups that they will actually be investigating the effects of positive and negative feedback on participation. When the first person returns to their group, they should provide only negative feedback, disregarding or disagreeing with any comments made by the person; the person's excuse for being late should be ignored or dismissed as "not good enough." When the second person returns, group members should express understanding regarding being late and provide positive feedback for any ideas presented. Direct students to begin their discussion of the assigned topic.

Next, provide instructions to the "latecomers," telling them that they will enter the classroom separately, with one returning three or four minutes before the other. Let them decide in their pairs who will return first. All should come up with reasons for being late to present to their groups. They should spend their waiting time discussing the topic. After the groups have been working for about five minutes, direct the first person from each group to return. After another five minutes, direct the rest of the students to rejoin their groups. Allow discussion to continue for another five minutes.

Debrief the activity by explaining its hidden purpose to the "latecomers" and by getting reports from the process observers, students who received negative feedback, and students who received positive feedback. Conclude with a general discussion of the effects of feedback.

PROCESS OBSERVER SHEET

<u>Directions</u>: Your job is to observe the group as it works. Try to watch how the group functions and what individuals <u>do</u> and <u>say</u> to help the group with its task. Resist the temptation to become involved--let the group work on its job while you watch how they work. The items below will give you specific things to watch for. If there is more than one process observer, you may wish to divide the items and group members between you. At the end of the task, you will be asked to report to the group on the questions below.

1.   What was the atmosphere in which the group worked? (Joyful, silly, tense, excited, etc.)

2.   How did the group reach decisions?

3.   How did the group handle conflict? (Humor, sarcasm, open confrontation, shouting, withdrawing, etc.)

4.   To what extent were all the members of the group involved in the task? Were there any procedures which helped people get involved?

5.   How did the group treat male/female differences?

6.   How did the group decide who would speak and when?

7.   How well did the group members listen to each other?

8.   Were there any leaders? How did they arise?

9.   How did the group delegate responsibility?

<u>Individually directed positive feedback</u>: Individually directed positive feedback can be helpful not only to the receiving individual but also to the entire group. Try to be as specific as possible (e.g., "Mary, your suggestion that the group try to isolate three ideas seemed to break the log jam.") Avoid individually directed negative feedback--chances are that all members of the group are aware of individual shortcomings, but these will seem less important and tend to disappear as the group recognizes and builds on the strengths of its members.

On a separate piece of paper, list the names of each of the group members, leaving a space for individually directed positive feedback.

COVER-UP GAME

Overview

We all react to situations in a manner that is determined by previous experiences. Scenes that appear real to one student will not to another. A human figure that one student sees as helpful may intimidate another student. Students are helped to clarify their feelings when they can analyze them in a relaxed, accepting environment. This activity provides a vehicle for students to explore diversity and their many responses to differences.

Objectives: At the conclusion of this activity, students will be better able to:

--list reasons why things should not be judged by their appearance

--explain what problems might result from judging things or people by their appearance

Grade Level: 2-8

Materials and Preparation: Collect an assortment of realistic pictures from news or picture magazines and mount them on construction paper. Pictures that work well in this activity are those that show people in activities that are often stereotyped as appropriate for people of one sex, race, or age and pictures showing cause-and-effect relationships. Cover one part of each picture with a small piece of paper; the part covered might be a person's face or the "cause" in a cause-and-effect picture.

Procedure

1. Display the pictures one at a time, asking students to hypothesize about what is shown in the covered portion of the picture. Ask questions to draw out students' opinions. For example: What type

Adapted from an activity by Jacob Eleasari and Kathy Bryant, in Helping Kids Learn Multi-Cultural Concepts: A Handbook of Strategies, by Michael G. Pasternak (Research Press, 1979), pp. 33-35. Used by permission.

of person is pictured? Why is that person in the picture? Why are they doing what the picture shows? What caused the event that is shown in the picture?

2. Accept all responses and post them on the chalkboard without evaluating them. Stereotypical evaluations are likely to emerge as the class analyzes the pictures. Figures engaged in certain activities will be prejudged to be either male or female, or associated with one ethnic group rather than another, or old rather than young.

3. After the class has had a chance to guess what's under the covered parts of the pictures, show the uncovered portions to them. Then help students identify why they responded as they did and how their assumptions affect behavior.

Follow-up

Encourage students to locate pictures to be used in this activity. For variety, project a frame from a filmstrip or a slide with the lens out of focus. Slowly adjust the focus while the students are trying to determine the content of the picture. Discuss how difficult it is to adjust your thinking once you believe you know what the picture is. Compare this characteristic with the manner in which prejudices keep our minds from making accurate assessments by blocking or keeping information out of focus.

FAMILIES IN THE WORLD OF MAKE-BELIEVE

Overview

Traditional fairy tales are rife with stereotypes of alternative family arrangements, such as adoption, foster care, and stepparenting. This activity permits students to analyze and compare treatments of these family forms in literature. The activity can also be extended to analysis of television programs that depict alternative family modes.

Objectives: At the end of this activity, students will be better able to:

--cite cases in which books have presented various types of families in a biased manner

--distinguish between positive and negative attitudes toward people in various types of families

Grade Level: K-6

Materials and Preparation: Obtain copies of the stories Cinderella, Hansel and Gretel, and Snow White. Be sure adequate chalkboard space or posting paper and marking pens are available.

Procedure

1. Point out to the class that stories and story books sometimes show certain kinds of people as being "bad," the villains. This is easy to understand because a story that had only "good guys" probably would not be very exciting. The problem is that some kinds of people are almost always shown as "bad" in make-believe stories. For example, in many fairy tales the "bad guys" are stepmothers or stepfathers.

2. Ask the class what a stepmother or stepfather is. Reinforce the point that a stepparent is a parent by marriage--for example, the man who marries your mother after she is divorced or widowed is your stepfather. Allow some time for discussion.

Activity by Daniel Gregg. Developed for the Adoption Builds Families Project of the Social Science Education Consortium. Used by permission.

3. Ask the class if they can think of stories that show stepmothers or stepfathers as being bad people. Accept all answers.

4. Divide the class into three groups. Give each group one of the stories. Ask the groups to read the books, looking for answers to the following questions, which should be written on the chalkboard:

--What words are used to describe the stepmother?

--What happens to the stepmother in the end?

Have each group write their responses on posting paper or the chalkboard and then share them with the rest of the class.

(If you have a primary-level class, you may wish to keep the students in a large group, reading the stories aloud to them. The above questions should be discussed at the end of each story.)

5. Have the students brainstorm reasons why some books treat stepparents in a negative way. Ask students to think about and discuss how a stepparent might feel while reading these stories to their stepchildren. How might the children feel?

Follow-up

In traditional fairy tales, stepparents--particularly stepmothers--were invariably cast as villains. In modern fairy tales, from The Sound of Music to The Brady Bunch, stepmothers are more likely to be candidates for sainthood. Ask students if they know of any television programs that present a positive view of stepparents. Discuss whether this view is always realistic. Could a too-positive view have negative effects as well? How would a stepmother feel if she was not as perfect as the mother on The Brady Bunch? How would stepchildren who watch that program expect their stepmothers to act?

Stepparents are not the only "different" parents whose portrayals have been distorted. Adoptive parents are often pictured as nearly too good to be true. Foster parents may be depicted as unselfish and noble or money-grubbing and exploitative. Single parents may also be stereotyped. Ask students to watch for portrayals of various family styles on television and report to the class on whether the members of these families are shown as "real" people who are both good and bad or whether they are shown as being either all "good" or all "bad."

IN-SIGHT GAME

Overview

This game is designed to encourage cooperation among group members while reinforcing content related to sex equity. The format can, however, be adapted to any content area; the teacher must only develop a new set of questions covering the desired content.

Objectives: At the conclusion of this activity, students will be better able to:

--work cooperatively with group members to solve a problem

--list examples of sex discrimination

--describe a variety of contributions made by women

Grade Level: 5-8

Materials and Preparation: You will need the following materials: a game board made on 20" x 24" poster board, a six-sided die, five or six playing pieces, 20 question cards on 8½" x 11" paper, a watch for timing penalties, tape or tacks to secure question cards, and a master question/answer sheet. If your class has not already studied the questions asked, you will also need reference materials.

To prepare for play, you will need to do the following:

1. Make the game board as shown on the next page, using 30 spaces. Intersperse numbers with penalty and bonus spaces.

2. Make 20 question cards on heavy 8½" x 11" paper. Number the cards, making the numbers large enough to be seen from a distance. Sample questions are provided at the end of the activity.

3. Determine the boundaries for the playing area; this can be the gymnasium, cafeteria, playground, etc. Secretly secure the questions in

---

Adapted from "Learning Experiences to Promote Sex Equity," by Sarah M. Butzin, Social Education 46, no. 1 (January 1982), pp. 48-53. Used by permission of the National Council for the Social Studies and Sarah M. Butzin.

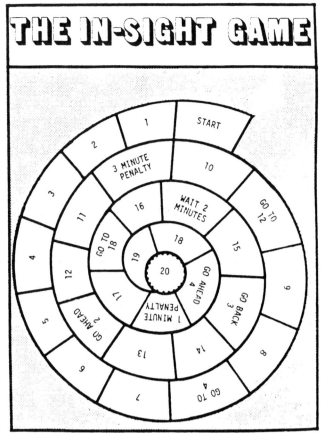

THE IN-SIGHT GAME

Illustrated by Dorothy Inman

a random fashion within the playing area; for example, questions might be tacked to trees or telephone poles, taped to walls or trash cans, etc. Be sure that questions are visible from a distance, but be clever in deciding where to put them. Do not hide any questions in out-of-sight places.

4. Select the home base (usually the classroom) and set up the game board.

Procedure

1. Divide the class into teams of four or five students. Each team should select a playing piece. Roll the die to determine the order in which teams are to proceed.

2. Read the following rules to the class:

--You must stay with your team. No answers will be accepted unless the entire team is present.

--Leave questions where they are. Do not remove a question or write on it.

--You must answer the question correctly before your team can roll the die again.

--If you break any rule, your team will be disqualified.

--The first team to reach 20 on the game board and give the correct answer to that question wins.

3. In the predetermined sequence, teams roll the die and move the playing piece to the proper square. If the square is a penalty or bonus square, students should follow the directions given. If the piece lands on a number, the team goes to find that question. When it finds the question, it must return with the answer. As soon as one team goes to find a question or enters a penalty period, the next team rolls the die.

4. When teams return with the answer to a question, check the answer. If it is correct, the team takes its next turn. If the answer is incorrect, additional attempts are permitted. For open-ended questions, accept any reasonable answer which the team agrees on and can defend. Checking reference materials can be permitted or disallowed according to the teacher's preference.

5. When one team reaches space 20 and answers that question correctly, reconvene the class and go over all the questions. Allow time for discussion of open-ended questions.

Sample Questions for In-Sight Game

1. Person X has a college degree and works as a secretary for $3.35 an hour. Person Y has a college degree and works as a secretary for the same company for $4.00 an hour. If they both work a 40-hour week, how much more does Person Y make than Person X? If X and Y are a different gender, which do you think is a man and which is a woman? Why? (Person Y makes $26 more.)

2. Last year, thousands of nurses graduated from college. Were there more men or women graduates? Why? (Women.)

3. Last year hundreds of doctors graduated from medical schools. Were there more men or women graduates? Why? (Men.)

4. Jack Nicklaus won four consecutive golf tournaments on the PGA tour. Nancy Lopez won four consecutive golf tournaments on the LPGA tour. Who earned more money? Why? (Nicklaus earned more.)

5. Who was Rachel Carson? (Environmentalist)

6. Who was Helen Sawyer Hogg? (Astronomer)

7. The average woman worker earns about 3/5 of what a man does. If a man were to earn $20,000, how much on the average would a woman make? Why? (A woman would make $12,000.)

8. What were women who struggled to get the right to vote for all women called? (Suffragettes or suffragists)

9. Have all adult Americans always had the right to vote? (No. Women could not vote until 1920.)

10. Which amendment to the U.S. Constitution gave women the right to vote? (19th)

11. Women are 78 percent of all clerical workers. What percent are men? Why? (22 percent)

12. Women are 5 percent of all craft workers. What percent are men? Why? (95 percent)

13. Whose picture is on the new one-dollar coin? Who was this person? (Susan B. Anthony was a leader in gaining women the right to vote.)

14. Name a female president of the United States. (None)

15. Name a female political leader in today's world. (For example: Indira Gandhi, India; Margaret Thatcher, United Kingdom)

16. At our school, how many teachers are female? How many administrators are female? (Answers will vary.)

17. How did Elizabeth Cady Stanton help women in America? (Helped women gain the right to vote)

18. One hundred people are elected to serve in the U.S. Senate. How many are men? Why? (98 are men.)

19. What does E.R.A. stand for? Give an argument for and against ratification. (Equal Rights Amendment)

20. Change this sentence to be inclusive of all persons and groups: We want peace for all mankind. (For example: We want peace for all people.)

Follow-up

Have students research other sex equity issues and develop additional questions based on their research. Present these questions in an activity based on a "College Bowl" format.

Section 3

UNDERSTANDING CITIZENSHIP

The activities in this section focus on rules and laws. The first two activities cover the same content--the need for rules or laws--at different levels of difficulty. "Why Rules?" is suitable for students in grades K-4, while "The Chowchilla Kidnapping Revisited" is intended for students in grades 5-8. The following three activities look at characteristics of a good law. "The Candy Game" helps primary students understand that rules should be "fair." "It's Against the Law" introduces students to the idea that laws develop in response to changing needs and thus sometimes become outdated. "Legal Confusion" points up the need for laws to be clear and understandable.

WHY RULES?

Overview

This activity has three phases. The first two involve students in two games, one with no rules and the other with rules that are explained as the game progresses, rather than in advance. The final phase takes students to the "Land of Confusion," where they learn the value of rules in solving societal problems. The three phases can be conducted one after the other, or can be spread over the course of the school day.

Objectives: At the conclusion of this activity, students will be better able to:

--explain the functions of rules

--describe why rules should be made specific before they need to be applied

--develop rules to remedy particular societal problems

Grade Level: K-4

Materials and Preparation: You will need two small balls, two pieces of chalk, masking tape, and several small bags of potato chips. Before the third phase of the activity, you will need to choose four group leaders, explain the group tasks to them, and provide any assistance needed in preparing for the group work.

Procedure

1. Ask six or eight students to go into the hall and divide themselves into two groups. Do not tell them how to organize themselves or what will happen when they come back.

Adapted from The Role of Law in a Free Society and the Rights and Responsibilities of Citizenship (Missouri State Bar Association and Missouri State Department of Elementary and Secondary Education, 1976), pp. c-21-22 and c-31-32. Used by permission of the Missouri Bar Committee on Citizenship Education.

2. After the two groups have gone outside, tell the rest of the class that you are going to throw a ball to each group when they return. As soon as you do that, the rest of the class should call out "go, go" and "win, win" and should clap and cheer. They should also watch what the group members do.

3. When the two groups return, put one group in one corner and the other group in another corner. Throw a ball to each group, signaling the rest of the class to begin cheering. Observe how the group members react.

4. Debrief this phase of the activity by asking the following questions: How did the group members feel? What did they need to know that they didn't know? How did the groups organize themselves? By sex, by size, or by friends? Were the groups equal in number? Would they have organized differently if they had known the rules of the game?

5. Tell the class that they are now going to play a game that does have rules. Pick 14 students who were not included in the original groups and divide them into two teams of seven students. Have the two teams stand in lines next to each other.

6. Tell the students that the object of the game is to pass a piece of chalk from the front of the line to the back and then to the front again before the other team does. Say "Go." Just as the students begin passing the chalk, yell "Stop."

7. Inform the teams that each member must go to a designated spot (the chalkboard) and return before passing the chalk on to the next person. Again tell the teams to start, but stop them after one team member has run to the spot and returned.

8. Tell the teams that a piece of masking tape should be wrapped around each player's left index finger with the sticky side out. The chalk can be passed by tape only. If hands touch the chalk, the team must start over. Again start the game and stop it before much progress is made.

9. Continue adding rules until the students object. At this point, stop the game and have the students take their seats.

10. Discuss the game with students, asking such questions as: Was the game fun? What would have helped make the game more fun? Can you think of other situations where it would help to know rules in advance?

Possible answers include in games and sports, in driving bicycles and automobiles, in purchasing goods and services, in manufacturing products, etc.

11. Before beginning phase 3 of the activity, you should select four group leaders and explain the group tasks to them. To begin this phase of the activity, tell the class that they are going to create a country called the "Land of Confusion." Divide the class into four groups called the mummers, noisemakers, organizers, and disorganizers. Explain that the group leader will tell them what their group's job is and that they can then plan and carry out activities that will fit that job. Tell them they will have 15 minutes to work on their jobs.

12. Circulate from group to group, ensuring that the leaders are explaining the group roles as specified below:

--Mummers remain quiet at all times. Communication is through sign language or note writing. They should undertake such quiet activities as silent reading, art projects, or working puzzles.

--Noisemakers create a lot of noise. They should pick very noisy activities. Provide several small bags of potato chips for the group to crunch and rattle.

--Organizers work to make the classroom orderly. They should pick such jobs as washing blackboards or straightening books or supply cases.

--Disorganizers should spend their time undoing the projects of the other groups--tearing up paper, cluttering the floor, drawing on the chalkboard, dumping out puzzles.

13. At the end of 15 minutes, have the class regroup and discuss the following questions: How did life in the "Land of Confusion" make students feel? What problems did they experience? How could those problems be dealt with? Could rules help solve the problems?

14. Have the students go back to their small groups and write a list of three rules that would help solve the problems of the "Land of Confusion." Let the groups share and compare their lists.

Follow-up

The entire class can express their ideas about rules through the creation of a class collage. Students can cut pictures representing rules from magazines and paste and glue them to large sheets of butcher paper. Discuss how the various pictures demonstrate the importance of rules.

THE CHOWCHILLA KIDNAPPING REVISITED

Overview

Rules and laws are guidelines established to maintain order in society. They are reflective of the values a particular society holds. This activity emphasizes understanding the origin of rules and laws based on the needs and values of society. A "minisociety" having no rules or laws is presented. Students are asked to identify their own values and see how rules and laws develop from them.

Objectives: At the conclusion of this activity, students will be better able to:

--define rule, law, and value

--identify a law written to enforce a particular group value

Grade Level: 5-8

Materials and Preparation: You will need copies of Handouts 3 and 4 for all the students.

Procedure

1. Tell students that the story they are about to hear is true. As you read, students should try to imagine themselves in the same situation.

On the afternoon of July 15, 1976, 31 children attending summer school at the Dairyland School got on the bus for their daily ride home. About 20 minutes later, after dropping off five children, the bus driver turned onto Avenue 21. Ahead was a white van with its driver's door open so that it crossed the line dividing the traffic lanes. The driver slowed the bus.

As the school bus neared the van, a man wearing a stocking mask and carrying a gun in each hand jumped out of the van and blocked the path of the bus. The bus driver

---

Adapted from TIPS: Crime Resistance Strategies, 6, by Martha Bass and others (Albemarle County and Charlottesville City Schools, 1978), pp. 1-11. Used by permission.

57

braked to a stop, and the masked man stepped to the window and told the bus driver to open the door. When he did, two more masked men jumped out of the van and followed the gunman onto the bus.

One of the masked men then drove the bus about a half mile along the road and down an incline, where a green van waited. The white van followed the bus along this route. The children were then unloaded into the two vans, which were hot and dark.

The vans drove for more than ten hours, with no food or restroom breaks. In the middle of the night, the vans left the paved road and traveled slowly over brush. Then they stopped.

The rear doors of the vans were opened and the bus driver and children were ordered to move into a tent-like structure. Each person was asked their name and age and an item of clothing was taken from them. They were then directed to climb down a manhole-sized opening which had a few feet of ladder sticking out of it.

When all the children had climbed down the ladder, the kidnappers handed down a roll of toilet paper, pulled up the ladder, and covered the access hole.

The driver and children examined their surroundings using the one flashlight the kidnappers had given them. They found that they were in a prison that looked like the interior of a trailer, about 27 feet long, 8 feet wide, and 8 feet high. Wire mesh covered the ceiling and walls. Against one wall stood a small pile of food--boxes of dry cereal, loaves of bread, bags of potato chips, a jar of peanut butter, and about a dozen large plastic jugs of water. Mattresses and box springs covered most of the floor space. Two toilets had been created over the wheels. Air could be felt coming through one of the two flexible pipes into the trailer and the sound of a fan could be heard from the pipe's far end . . .

2.   Distribute copies of Handout 3. Have students rank the items from most important (10) to least important (1). Write their rankings on the board to determine the overall class choices. To get the totals, follow this example: if 15 students value air as the top priority (15 x 10 = 150), 5 rank it as second choice (5 x 9 = 45), and 5 rank it third (5 x 8 = 40), then air would receive a total of 235.

3.   Review the following definitions with students:

--rule: a written or oral guide that tells us how to act.

58

--law: a set of rules by which a particular group or community regulates the conduct of the people within it. Laws are usually made by governments and can also be called statutes or ordinances.

4. Discuss reasons why rules and laws are necessary. Be sure the following points are mentioned:

--to help settle disputes. At some time, we all get into arguments. At home we may argue over use of the TV, over whose turn it is to wash the dishes, over who left the water on and flooded the bathroom. We get into disputes outside the home too. Two neighbors may argue because one's dog barks all night and keeps the other awake. Two drivers in an auto accident may disagree over who was at fault.

--to protect us. We have laws to prevent factories from dumping poisons into a town's water supply. We have laws to help set safety standards, such as building codes. We also have laws to keep us healthy, such as quality standards for food.

--to help guide our daily activities. A law defines how to behave. It tells you precisely what to do--or what not to do. It also tells you what to expect if you do not obey the law. Clearly not all laws are good. A law can be very unjust and very harmful. But when people know how they are expected to behave and what to expect from others, few disagreements arise. When disagreements and conflict do arise, laws give us a way to reach a settlement.

5. Ask students what would happen to the "minisociety" caught in the kidnapping situation if there were no rules. Possible answers will vary widely but might include such results as one student's eating all the food, fighting, hoarding of supplies, etc.

6. Review the following definition:

--value: an ideal or belief one holds important. A value is manifested through actions and behavior.

7. Provide students with copies of Handout 4. Divide the class into four or five small groups. Have the groups read the worksheet and place an "X" in front of the solution the group thinks is best in each of the six situations. Point out that values are the influencing factor: Is food more important than escape, water more important than air? Once they have made a value choice for each situation, ask the groups to write a law that would protect each of the values chosen.

This portion of the activity demonstrates how rules and laws are formed. For instance, if a society decides that education is important, then it writes a law that says all children must go to school until a certain age. However, if a society decides work is more important than education, then it writes a law allowing children to apply for a work-release permit.

8. Have the class come back together and compare their value choices and the laws they have written. Write the laws on the board and have students vote for three that will govern the group while they are held captive. These three laws should then be written under "Community Laws" on the worksheet. In making a group decision on the choices and formation of rules and laws, the students will need to compromise and accept majority rule. The class should compare the three "community laws" with the original "Life Necessities" ranking to see if the laws protect the items that the students originally chose as most important.

9. If students are interested, read the conclusion of the Chowchilla story:

> The children gulped the water, used the toilets, and tore into the food. Within an hour, the food was gone. After 12 hours, only three containers of water remained.
>
> After considering how much more captivity the children could stand and what might happen if they were caught trying to escape, the bus driver decided to make an attempt. By piling up mattresses, the captives were able to reach the entrance hole. Moving the lid, breaking through a large box placed over the entrance hole, and digging through the dirt in the box took many hours of hard work. But at last the driver and children were free.
>
> Help was found and the police were called. Soon the children were on their way home. Police investigation led to the arrest of the kidnappers, three men in their early 20s.

Follow-up

Give students copies of Handout 5 to complete. Ask students: If you were allowed to take one item with you into the buried prison, what would it be? Each student should write a paragraph explaining his or her choice.

DIRECTIONS: You are trapped in the underground prison. You want to escape. You want to survive. But, you must decide how to control behavior and rations to maximize your chances.

Rank the following items in order of importance from 1-10. 10 is MOST important — 1 is LEAST important.

_____ food

_____ use of flashlight

_____ water

_____ air

_____ limited space

_____ privacy (restrooms)

_____ sleep (rest)

_____ escape

_____ entertainment

_____ clothing

Choices for Survival

1. Your food is limited. Everybody is very hungry. Would you...
   ____ ration it to last over as long a time period as possible?
   ____ let everybody have one good meal and then begin to ration?
   ____ decide who is stronger and who is weaker and let the weaker ones have the food they need first?

   Law:

2. The air coming through two pipes in the roof is becoming very thin. You would...
   ____ limit talking because it uses up more air.
   ____ let people take turns being near the air pipes.
   ____ try to make the air holes larger even though you risk a cave-in.

   Law:

3. There are 12 gallon jugs of water and 27 people trapped. The temperature is becoming hotter and hotter. You know that without water the body will begin to dehydrate. You would...
   ____ decide who are the stronger ones in the group and let them have the water because their strength would be needed the most in escape attempts.
   ____ let each person decide for himself how much he needs to stay healthy.
   ____ give one capful of water to each person every hour.

   Law:

4. Your only source of light is one flashlight with two extra batteries. You have no idea how long you will be held captive. Would you...
   ____ limit the use of the flashlight to so many minutes an hour?
   ____ use the flashlight only to look for escape possibilities?
   ____ use the flashlight a lot at first to get to know your surroundings and to calm the kids who are afraid of the dark and when the first battery is used up, then start to limit its use?

   Law:

5. You know you were lowered into this "prison" through a hole in the ground. You can hear the roof of the trailer creaking under the weight above it. Already it has begun to cave in and a little dirt is sprinkling down on you and the other captives. Trying to tunnel out may risk a cave-in from the earth above. Would you...
   ____ not risk a cave-in and wait to be rescued?
   ____ wait at least until the food and water are gone and then try to escape?
   ____ attempt escape even though you risk a cave-in and the kidnappers may be waiting for you on the surface?

   Law:

6. Many of your friends are becoming upset and afraid they will never get out and perhaps will die in this place. They are crying. You would...
   ____ try to make everyone happier by encouraging singing, etc.
   ____ get angry at the ones who are crying because they are using up valuable air.
   ____ decide to keep the flashlight on all the time because it will make them less scared.

   Law:

COMMUNITY LAWS:

1. _____

2. _____

3. _____

Trapped

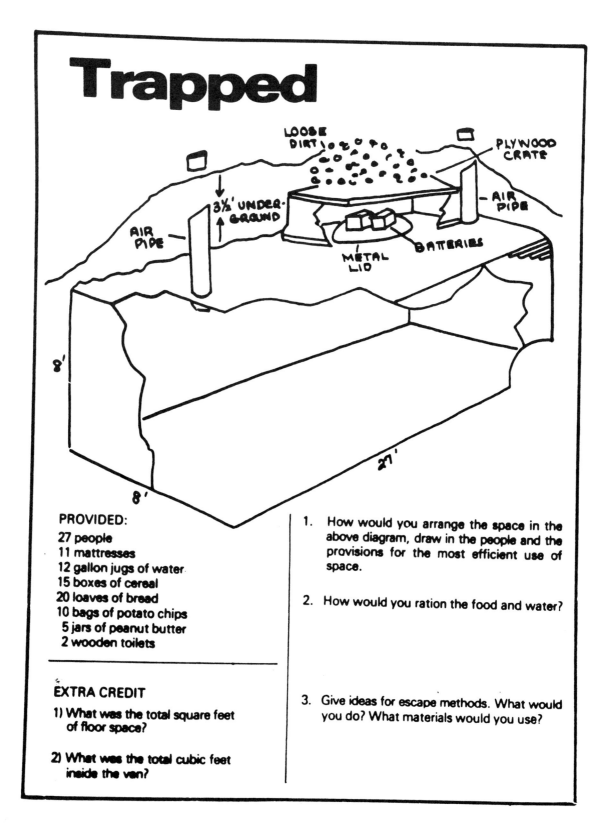

PROVIDED:

27 people
11 mattresses
12 gallon jugs of water
15 boxes of cereal
20 loaves of bread
10 bags of potato chips
5 jars of peanut butter
2 wooden toilets

EXTRA CREDIT

1) What was the total square feet of floor space?

2) What was the total cubic feet inside the van?

1. How would you arrange the space in the above diagram, draw in the people and the provisions for the most efficient use of space.

2. How would you ration the food and water?

3. Give ideas for escape methods. What would you do? What materials would you use?

THE CANDY GAME

Overview

This activity--a game--demonstrates that rules should not be capricious and arbitrary. It also demonstrates that the way in which laws are made can influence their "fairness."

Objectives: At the conclusion of this activity, students will be better able to:

--explain why rules should not be arbitrary

--suggest ways of enacting laws that would enhance the possibility that the laws will be fair

Grade Level: 1-6

Materials and Preparations: You will need an equal number of pieces of two kinds of wrapped candies, such as striped peppermints and caramels. The total number of pieces should be equal to the number of students in your class.

Procedure

1. Tell students that you are going to play the "Candy Game." Pass out the candy, giving each student one piece. Point out that all students have equal resources--one piece of candy. The winner of the game will be the student who ends up with the most pieces of candy.

2. Tell all students having caramels that they must give their candy to students having peppermints and that they are now out of the game.

Adapted from The Role of Law in a Free Society and the Rights and Responsibilities of Citizenship (Missouri State Bar Association and Missouri State Department of Elementary and Secondary Education, 1976), p. c-27. Used by permission of the Missouri Bar Committee on Citizenship Education.

3. Pair off all students still in the game and tell the taller one in each pair to give their candy to the shorter student. The taller students are now out of the game.

4. Tell all right-handed students holding candy to line up to your right; all left-handed students holding candy should line up to your left. Tell the right-handed students to hand their candy to left-handed students and leave the game.

5. Continue selecting arbitrary categories (e.g., color of clothing, number of children in family, color of eyes, straight or curly hair) until one child ends up with all the candy. Declare him or her to be the "Candy Game Champion."

6. Ask students what the fairest rule for ending the game would be. Begin with the child who has the candy and let others offer additional suggestions. Follow the suggestion most children will find to be fair--redistributing one piece of candy to each student.

7. Discuss whether the rules of the game were fair. Ask: Who made the rules? Did the children have any "say" in the rules? Would the rules have been better if the children had written them?

8. Discuss whether anyone tried to break the rules by putting candy in their pockets or pretending they fit into a category that did not actually describe them. Discuss who should enforce rules. Ask: What is the responsibility of people in a game to tell about cheating? What is the responsibility of children and adults when they see rules or laws broken?

Follow-up

As a follow-up, focus a discussion on students' feelings when they were eliminated from the game for totally arbitrary reasons. Were they angry? Hurt? Frustrated? If possible, lead students to draw the connection between their reactions to the rules of the game and reactions of groups against whom discriminatory laws are enacted.

IT'S AGAINST THE LAW

Overview

In this activity, students examine humorous laws to determine what conditions in society might have led to their enactment. The aim is to help students understand that laws develop in response to particular individual or societal needs and thus change as needs change.

Objectives: At the conclusion of this activity, students will be better able to:

--understand the social value of particular laws

--realize that laws develop in response to the changing needs of citizens and thus vary from one group to another and from one time to another

Grade Level: 4-8

Materials and Preparation: Make seven copies of Handout 6.

Procedure

1. Divide the class into seven groups and give each group a copy of the handout. Assign three of the laws listed on the handout to each group. Ask the group to read their laws and figure out why each might have been passed. Ask them to consider what conditions in society they think might have led people to write such a law and what conditions today might force society to keep, rescind, amend, or ignore the law. Give the groups 15 minutes to complete their analysis.

2. Ask each group to select a group reporter and have that person present the group's ideas to the class.

Adapted from Words Into Action: A Classroom Guide to Children's Citizenship Education, by Joseph D'Amico and others (Research for Better Schools, 1980), pp. 35-36. Activity developed by John True, Huron Junior High School, Northglenn, CO. Used by permission.

3. Conclude the activity with a brief general discussion of how laws evolve as the needs of individuals and societies change. In the future, what laws that now seem very sensible might appear foolish?

Follow-up

Have each class member write down a rule or law which he/she must follow at home, in school, or in the community which seems to be a silly one. Ask each student to present his/her rule to the class, explaining why it is silly. Challenge other students to provide valid reasons for the enactment and enforcement of these rules and laws.

LOONY LAWS

1.   In Nicholas County, West Virginia, no minister shall tell a funny story from the pulpit.

2.   In Compton, California, dancing cheek to cheek is prohibited.

3.   Beanshooters are forbidden by law in Arkansas.

4.   It is illegal to hunt or shoot camels in Arizona.

5.   In Los Angeles, a customer of a meat market is prohibited by city ordinance from poking a turkey to see if it is tender.

6.   In Springfield, Massachusetts, it is against the law to ride on the roof of your automobile.

7.   In Lake Charles, Louisiana, law makes it illegal to let a rain puddle remain in your front yard for more than twelve hours.

8.   In Hanford, California, people may not interfere with children jumping over water puddles.

9.   It is against the law in Pueblo, Colorado, to raise or permit a dandelion to grow within the city limits.

10.   In Walden, New York, it is illegal to give a drink of water to anyone unless you have a permit.

11.   It is against the law in Illinois for a conductor to collect fares without his hat on.

12.   In Bradford, Connecticut, it's against the law to appear on the street unless covered from shoulder to knee.

13.   It is against the law to slap a man on the back in Georgia.

14.   In Vermont it is illegal to whistle under water.

15.   All taxicabs must carry a broom and shovel in the District of Columbia.

16.   In Key West, Florida, turtle racing is prohibited.

17.   In Fort Madison, Iowa, law requires the fire department to practice 15 minutes before attending a fire.

18.   It's against the law to gargle in public in Louisiana.

19.   Rochester, New York, firemen must wear neckties on duty.

20.   In Kentucky it is illegal to sleep in a restaurant.

21.   In Rochester, Michigan, anyone bathing in public must first have his suit inspected by a police officer.

LEGAL CONFUSION

Overview

Our behavior is most effectively guided by laws which are clearly communicated to us. In this lesson, students recognize that some laws are communicated in such a way that they can easily be misunderstood; they examine the consequences of such unclear laws.

Objectives: At the conclusion of this activity, students will be better able to:

--tell why laws must be clearly stated to effectively guide people's behavior

--distinguish between laws that are clearly and vaguely communicated

--design procedures for clearly communicating laws to people in given situations

--rewrite vaguely written laws so that their intent is more clearly communicated

Grade Level: 5-8

Materials and Preparation: You will need copies of Handouts 7 and 8 for all the students.

Procedure

1. Distribute copies of Handout 7. Direct students to read the story and follow the directions.

2. After students have had sufficient time to complete the worksheet, discuss their responses. Point out the confusion that

Adapted from Learning About Law: A Law-Related Instructional Unit for Children in Grades 5 and 6, by David T. Naylor (Ohio State Bar Association, 1980), pp. 28-31. Used by permission.

unclear signs can create. (Note: These are actual signs that the authors observed in Ohio. "No Standing" prohibits cars from stopping or parking in the designated area. It does not refer to people. The city of Cincinnati has decided to replace these signs with "No Parking" signs because of the confusion created. "Don't Mow Trees" was observed on a hillside along an interstate highway. It cautioned those who mowed the grass to avoid the area because seedlings, planted to retard erosion, were planted there.)

3. Distribute Handout 8 to students. Have students work in pairs to complete the activity.

4. Lead a class discussion about the three laws on the handout. Emphasize the confusion created by unclear laws. Help students understand the reasons for clear and understandable laws. (Note: In Law A, must the dog or the owner of the dog be on a leash? In Law B, what is an object? Does this law prohibit playing catch, launching a paper airplane, or tossing a paper clip into a wastepaper basket? In Law C, are all bees prohibited or only beehives? If persons are permitted to have beehives in a neighboring town, what happens if some of their bees fly into this town?)

Follow-up

Students might enjoy making up signs that illustrate rules for different parts of the classroom. Some of these could be humorous; for example, a "Children Crossing" sign in the hallway, a "No Standing" sign at the teacher's desk, etc. Encourage students to illustrate the signs with cartoon characters and captions.

As an alternative, have students write confusing rules for the classroom. They should attempt to write one confusing rule for every regular rule they follow in the room; for example, "No Writing on Desks" could mean no writing of any kind, whether on paper or not. After students have finished their "unclear" rules, divide the class into groups of three. Let students share their rules within their groups. Each group should nominate the three most creative ideas from their group. A poster of these unclear rules, along with their clear and understandable counterparts, could be displayed in the classroom.

SIGNS CAN BE CONFUSING

Brenda, a second-grader, and her family decided to go to the zoo. As they drove from their home to the city, they passed many signs along the way. Brenda noticed that some of the signs were easy to understand. But other signs were not very clear and she found them very confusing. Below are some of the signs that Brenda saw. Next to each sign is what Brenda thought it meant. Do you agree with her? If not, put a line through what Brenda said and write in what you think the sign means.

Brenda thought this meant, "Don't move!"

_____

_____

Brenda thought this meant, "Only running or crawling allowed here!"

_____

_____

Brenda thought this meant, "Don't mow the trees!" (That's right, don't mow the trees!)

_____

_____

Brenda thought this meant, "Make your fires here."

_____

_____

Brenda thought this meant, "Give up!"

_____

_____

Brenda thought this meant, "Kids who live around here run very slowly."

_____

_____

LAWS SHOULD BE STATED CLEARLY

Just as some signs may not be clear, laws themselves are sometimes unclear. The three laws below are not very well written. Rewrite them so that they are clear and understandable.

LAW A: No dog shall be in a public place with its owner on a leash.

          Questions: 1. What does this law permit or prohibit?
                    2. Rewrite this law so that its meaning is clear.

_____

_____

LAW B: No stones or other objects shall be thrown in any way, at any time, any place in the city.

          Questions: 1. What does this law permit or prohibit?
                    2. Rewrite this law so that its meaning is clear.

_____

_____

LAW C: Bees are not permitted within city limits.

          Questions: 1. What does this law permit or prohibit?
                    2. Rewrite this law so that its meaning is clear.

_____

_____

Section 4

UNDERSTANDING GEOGRAPHY

The activities in this section cover topics ranging from the most basic geographic terms to complex questions of land use. The first activity, "Making Mountains," involves kindergarten and first-grade students in modeling landforms and using their models in creative play. The second, third, and fourth activities are all mapping tasks, ranging from students' mapping themselves to mapping an unfamiliar room arrangement explored while blindfolded. The fifth activity, "No Place to Play," focuses on complicated issues involved in determining where recreational facilities should be located. The final activity, "The Flume," describes a teaching device and game format that can be used to reinforce any social studies content; as described here, the activity focuses on energy.

MAKING MOUNTAINS

Overview

This activity includes two key parts: making models of landforms and playing with the models. The play portion of the activity is part of the instructional experience. Integrating their representations into block and manipulative play will provide students with opportunities to understand site concepts and to see the relationships between different site characteristics.

Objectives: At the conclusion of this activity, students will be better able to:

--understand site concepts (landforms and bodies of water)
--explain how models are used to represent real objects

Grade Level: K-1

Materials and Preparation: You will need a number of large cake pans of tin plate or aluminum foil; students may be able to bring some from home. You will also need clay or molding dough and varnish or lacquer. Molding dough can be made as follows. Mix 2 cups of table salt and 2/3 cup water in a saucepan, stirring until the mixture is well-heated (two to four minutes). Do not boil. Remove from heat and add a mixture of 1 cup cornstarch and ½ cup cold water. Stir quickly. The mixture, which will keep indefinitely if stored in plastic bags, should have the consistency of stiff dough. You will also need magazines and scissors or pictures of various landforms and bodies of water.

From Kindergarten Social Studies Program: Teacher's Resource Guide, by Charles L. Mitsakos (Chelmsford Public Schools, 1976), p. 23. Used by permission.

<u>Procedure</u>

1. Write a number of topographical terms on the chalkboard and briefly define each. The sophistication of the terms listed and explanations given will depend on whether students have had any previous introduction to such terms. Appropriate terms for students with no previous experience include mountain, island, peninsula, cliff, hill, plain, river, lake, and bay.

2. Distribute magazines and scissors and ask students to look for and cut out pictures illustrating the terms discussed. Post the pictures around the room.

3. Working in pairs, have the children model representations of these topographical phenomena in large cake pans, using modeling clay or molding dough. Allow the models to dry thoroughly, then coat them with lacquer or varnish.

4. When the varnish has dried, allow the children to integrate the models into block structures. Allow children to bring in some small plastic boats and to use water with their representations where appropriate. Encourage students who become interested in the structures to build bridges over rivers or docking facilities along the edge of the lake. These activities will help students understand site concepts and see the relationships between different site characteristics. Allow the play to be carried over for several days, if possible.

<u>Follow-up</u>

Discuss with students the topographical features in your region. If possible, arrange a field trip in which students can see several examples of features studied in this activity.

THE "ME" MAP

Overview

This activity introduces students to maps and such important map concepts as relative location and symbols through a map of the territory most familiar to them—themselves.

Objectives: At the conclusion of this activity, students will be better able to:

--understand that a map shows location

--locate body parts in relative position on an outline drawing of a body

--use symbols as representations of actual parts of the body

Grade Level: K-2

Materials and Preparation: You will need butcher paper, pencils, black crayons, paint, and brushes.

Procedure

1. Ask students if they have ever seen their parents using a road map. Ask: Why were they using a road map?

2. Tell students that they are going to have a chance to make maps of their own bodies, showing where the various parts are. Discuss what should go on the maps of their bodies. As children make suggestions, write them on the chalkboard. Then have the children suggest symbols to represent the parts of the body. For example,

Eyes ○ ○	Knees ⌒
Nose △	Waist ≋
Mouth ‿	Ankle ////
Elbows ▢	Wrist ∿∿

From There's More than the Three R's to Those Early Years, by Dorothy J. Skeel and Ronald E. Sterling, paper presented at the annual meeting of the National Council for the Social Studies, November 1978. Used by permission of the authors.

3. Have the children work in pairs, taking turns lying on the butcher paper while their partner uses a black crayon to make their body outline.

4. Refer the children to the chart on the board, instructing them to draw in the symbols to represent the location of the various body parts. Explain that the chart on the board is the key or legend for their maps.

5. Allow children to paint their "Me" maps. Display the maps around the classroom.

Follow-up

Encourage students to become aware of maps and their uses by creating a bulletin board display with a variety of maps. Be sure each map is labeled. Help students examine the symbols used.

MAP QUARTERS

Overview

This simple activity is extremely effective in developing the concepts of scale and symbolization. Working separately, groups of students each map a portion of a large picture. While the results are often quite funny, they also provide the opportunity to observe the impact of using different symbols and scale.

Objectives: At the conclusion of this activity, students will be better able to:

--describe the effect of using different scales on maps of the same area

--use a variety of symbols to represent pictured items

Grade Level: 2-4

Materials and Preparation: You will need a large picture showing a scene that could be appropriately mapped by students. Divide the picture into quarters, outlining and numbering each quarter. Post the picture on the wall. Students will need paper, drawing materials, and tape.

Procedure

1. Draw students' attention to the picture you have posted, briefly discussing the pictured scene.

2. Divide the class into four groups, assigning one quarter of the picture to each group. All the members of a particular group must draw maps of the quarter of the picture assigned to their group. The

Adapted from Map and Compass Skills for the Elementary School, Instructional Activities Series IA/E-9, by Robert P. Larkin and Paul K. Grogger (National Council for Geographic Education, 1975). Used by permission.

groups should be as physically separated as the space available allows, so the students cannot see what members of other groups are drawing. Students can use crayons, pens, pencils, and any size paper they choose.

3. When students have finished their mapping, each must find three students who have done the other three quarters of the picture. Each group of four students should tape their maps together to create the complete picture. Groups should post their maps around the room.

4. Allow time for students to examine all the maps. The results of the match-up are very interesting and often funny. Conduct a discussion of the symbols used and the impact of using different scales.

Follow-up

Have students collect maps of your community or state drawn to several different scales. Ask students to compare the information provided on the various maps. What are the advantages of using a particular scale? The disadvantages?

BE A GEOGRAPHER

Overview

This exploration game is designed to open up the classroom to geographic exploration and discovery. The game simulates what it might have been like to explore as Columbus, with limited sight capabilities, crude navigational devices, and the dilemma of deciding how to map the "land" they discover.

Objectives: At the conclusion of this activity, students will be better able to:

--describe some of the difficulties faced by Columbus in sailing to and mapping the New World

--use a map to show the relative location of items in a room

Grade Level: 4-8

Materials and Preparation: This game can be conducted in the classroom or any other room. Before the students arrive, you will need to rearrange the tables, desks, and other furniture in the room (see sketches below), pull the shades so that outside light does not enter the room, and place a small radio next to the door through which the students will enter the room. You will also need a blindfold, paper, and pencil for each student.

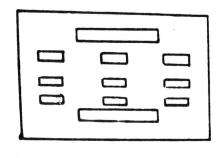

original room

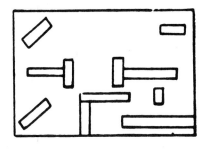

rearranged room

Adapted from Children are Geographers: Explorations in Space, Instructional Activities Series IA/E-12, by O. Fred Donaldson (National Council for Geographic Education, 1975), pp. 2-3. Used by permission.

Procedure

1. Meet the students outside of the room; do not allow anyone who is going to participate to go into the room. Explain the following rules:

--Each student is to make a map of the room as it is.

--Students are to put on their blindfolds outside the room and keep them on while in the room.

--Paper and pencil are left outside the room. Students can come out as many times as they wish, take off their blindfolds, and map what they "saw."

--While they are in the room, they walk around and "see" things by touching them.

--They are to listen to the radio to guide themselves back out of the room.

2. Set a time limit and direct students to begin their work.

3. When the time has expired, reconvene the class--without blindfolds--in the classroom. Allow a few minutes for students to compare their maps to the actual arrangement.

4. Discuss with students how their experience was similar to what it might have been like to explore as Columbus. Both the students and Columbus had limited sight capabilities, one seeing as far as the telescopic technology of his time allowed, the others seeing as far as the ends of their fingers. Both had to navigate--one by the stars, the other by radio sound--to find home. They faced a common dilemma when "land" was hit. Were they interested in the general outlines or the details of the coastline? What consequences resulted from the choices made? Did students who opted to map details spend valuable time mapping the details of a dead end? Did those interested only in general outlines miss significant land passages? How would students have felt charting a totally unexplored area rather than a familiar room?

Follow-up

Show students early maps of North America. Ask students to identify differences between these maps and modern maps. Discuss possible reasons for these differences.

NO PLACE TO PLAY

Overview

   As the population continues to expand, the location of recreational areas for the public has taken on increasing importance. How can children be made aware that every public recreational decision involves a value choice, often to the detriment of someone's rights? How can children be led to analyze the adequacy, equity, and efficiency of public decisions and the value priorities reflected in them? What does a teacher do to sensitize youngsters to the interplay of political, social, economic, spatial, and even historical factors involved in public recreational decisions? This activity uses a case study to involve students in these questions. The activity can be completed in a relatively short period or be expanded over several hours.

   Objectives: At the conclusion of this activity, students will be better able to:

   --identify how decisions regarding land use reflect community values

   --list at least three factors impinging on public decisions regarding land use

   --participate in group problem-solving processes

Grade Level: 5-8

   Materials and Preparation: You will need to make copies of Handout 9 for all the students.

Procedure

   1.   Distribute copies of Handout 9 and give students time to read the case study description, or read the description aloud. Explain

---

Adapted from No Place to Play: Valuing Dilemmas in the Choice of Recreational Sites, Instructional Activities Series IA/E-7, by Peter H. Martorella and Jack Madden (National Council for Geographic Education, 1975). Used by permission.

that the class will be working in small groups representing the four areas of Urbo to develop proposals for new recreational facilities. They will then present those proposals to the class, and the class as a whole will vote on the proposal.

2. Using the basic information provided on the handout, ask the class to illustrate the characteristics of Urbo with a graphic sketch. Once the class reaches consensus on a sketch, it should be used as the common reference point for the class.

3. Divide the class into four groups, assigning each to represent one of the four areas of Urbo. Working within their groups, students should determine what sort of recreational facilities should be provided, decide where the recreational facilities should be located, and list changes or consequences that are likely to occur if their recommendations are put into action. Students should be able to present a rationale for each of their decisions. Set a fixed amount of time for the small-group work; this can be as little as a half-hour or as much as two class periods, depending on the time you have available.

4. At the end of the set time, have each group make a brief presentation to the class on its recommendations. If time permits, let the other groups question the presenter. When all groups have made their presentations, the class should vote on the options. Remember, a majority vote is required to adopt any one recommendation. If no decision is reached and time is available, allow the students to negotiate a compromise solution.

5. Discuss how the exercise demonstrates the various factors that impinge on land use decisions, as well as how such decisions reflect community values.

Follow-up

Once students have been involved in planning for which variables have been controlled, they may consider recreational concerns in their own community. Field experiences could be used to better acquaint students with existing facilities and with the feasibility of proposed solutions. Also, community and student attitudes on recreational issues could be sampled through simple interview-questionnaire techniques.

Using a map of their local area as a starting point, students might be asked to deal with questions similar to the following ones:

--Where are the public recreational facilities in our community located?

--Are these facilities easy for all groups within the community to get to? If not, who suffers the most? Why do you suppose the facilities have been located where they are?

--Ideally, what should recreational facilities in our community be like and where should they be located?

--Who would be affected and in what ways by the recommendations that we have made? What groups might support and what groups might oppose our recommendations? Why?

--What do our recreational recommendations and the existing recreational conditions in our community tell us about what we think is important and what we are willing to sacrifice for it?

THE CASE OF URBO

Urbo is a city that has doubled in population in recent years. The fine parks, playgrounds, and public recreational areas that were once the pride of all its citizens no longer can hold all of the people who wish to use them. And all ages of people now have more free time than ever for recreation. The residents all over the city are complaining that there are not enough open public areas for sports, play, picnicking, or other recreational activities, and they wish to take some action. Everyone agrees that more public recreational areas are needed, but no one is sure where they should be located or what kinds of materials and activities they should have.

Urbo covers a region of approximately 150 square miles, and, like most cities, is made up of a variety of different types of people with different recreational needs. In general, however, you may consider most of the people in Urbo as living in four different areas of the city, and as having the characteristics listed below.

NORTHSIDERS

Resident Income:	Very high, well above average
Property Costs:	Very high
Industries:	None
Stores:	Few
Major Traffic Arteries:	Very few
People Per Square Mile:	Very few
Type of Inhabitants:	Mostly families with children; very few single adults

SOUTHSIDERS

Resident Income:	Average
Property Costs:	Average
Industries:	None
Stores:	Few
Major Traffic Arteries:	Very few
People Per Square Mile:	Few
Type of Inhabitants:	Mostly older families whose children have already left home; only a few single adults

EASTSIDERS

Resident Income:	Less than average
Property Costs:	Low
Industries:	Many
Stores:	Many
Major Traffic Arteries:	Many
People Per Square Mile:	Very many
Type of Inhabitants:	Mostly families with children; also many single adults

WESTSIDERS

Resident Income:	Average
Property Costs:	Average
Industries:	Few
Stores:	Many
Major Traffic Arteries:	Average number
People Per Square Mile:	Average number
Type of Inhabitants:	Mostly middle-aged families with few children left at home; only a few single adults

Your task: You are to make recommendations for additional public recreational plans with sites, materials, and activities to serve all of the people from the four areas of Urbo. Any recommendations that you make must be approved in an election by a majority of all of the voters of Urbo. It is important to remember that there are no more open spaces in Urbo, so that any new recreational areas that you recommend will require the removal of some citizens' homes or stores.

THE FLUME

Overview

This activity presents an adaptable design for reinforcing content. Adaptable designs are structural formats that can be used repeatedly with different concepts/skills. This activity focuses on modern energy issues, but teachers could just as easily use it to reinforce knowledge about inventors or early explorers. Students have gone agog over this design. True, the manner in which students receive immediate reinforcement is gimmicky, but it works. Why argue with success?

Objectives: At the conclusion of this activity, students will be better able to:

--define key terms related to energy

Grade Level: 4-6

Materials and Preparation: Obtain four cigar boxes (or milk cartons) for use as "flumes." To prepare a flume, cut two ½"-wide slots in the box, as shown in the diagram. Cut two strips of aluminum foil or oaktag using the following dimensions: 2" wide by approximately 12½" long, and 2" wide by approximately 9½" long. Place the strips in the box so as to form a chute. Bend the strip ends at least ½" around the upper and lower edges of the cutout slots. Fasten with a durable cement. Decorate the box to give it a "personality." Cut a number of cards measuring 3" x 1". Larger cards may not fit through the chute. Prepare several sets of question cards. Each card should have a question and red dot on one side and the answer on the other side. Sample questions are provided at the end of the activity.

Adapted from Motivational Use of Adaptable Designs in Reinforcing Geographic-Social Studies Content, by Randall A. Pelow, paper presented at the annual meeting of the National Council for Geographic Education, 1981, pp. 8-9. Used by permission.

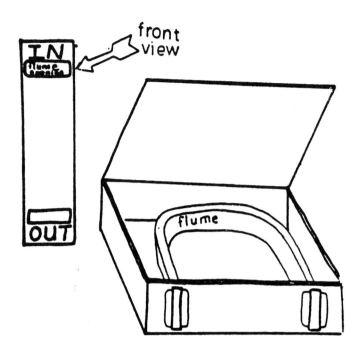

Procedure

1. Divide the class into eight teams; two teams should gather around a table or group of desks. Give each pair of two teams a flume and a stack of question cards. Direct them to place the questions on the table with the red dot (question side) up.

2. Teams should flip a coin to see who starts first. The team starting first looks at the first question card, reading the question aloud. Both teams should caucus and discuss the question, arriving at a consensus answer without letting the other team hear their discussion. The first team states its answer aloud, places the card in the flume with the red dot up, and then checks the right answer. If they were right, they score one point; if they were wrong, the second team has the opportunity to answer the question. If they give the right answer, they score one point. Use of reference materials in answering questions can be allowed or disallowed according to the teacher's preference.

3. The game proceeds, with teams alternating at having the first try at a question, until all the questions have been answered. The team from each pair scoring the most points wins.

Sample Questions

1. Name three fossil fuels. (Coal, natural gas, and oil)
2. Electricity can be created by fast-moving water. What is this energy source called? (Hydroelectric power)
3. Another energy source involves water heated under the earth's surface. What is this form of energy called? (Geothermal energy)
4. Changing plant material into energy is known as _____. (Biomass)
5. Name the system in which the design of a building provides for the collection, transfer, and storage of heat energy to air and water. (Passive solar heating)
6. Which energy source is cheaper--nuclear, oil, or geothermal? (Geothermal)
7. About how many years did it take nature to make coal? (1,000,000 years)
8. How long does it take to burn a pound of coal in an average-size home furnace? (Less than five minutes)
9. What part of the world's energy does the United States consume? (33 percent)
10. Who uses more energy--poor people, people of average wealth, or rich people? (In general, rich people)
11. Generating energy by splitting a nucleus is called _____. (Fission)

Follow-up

The flumes can be placed in learning centers with a range of question cards for students to use in independent study and review.

Section 5

UNDERSTANDING HISTORY

The first activity in this section, "There's an Old Trunk in My Attic," help students develop a historical sense; writing skills are also emphasized in this activity. The remaining activities focus on topics that often do not receive extensive coverage in standard text materials. "My Folks Came in a Covered Wagon" uses primary source documents to teach about children's experiences on the American frontier. "Should Men Have the Vote?" provides a means of enlivening study of the suffrage movement. The final two activities in the section--"What Would You Pack?" and "The Land of Milk and Honey"--examine the immigrant experience in the late 1800s and early 1900s.

THERE'S AN OLD TRUNK IN MY ATTIC

Overview

This activity does not present specific historic content. Rather, it helps students develop a sense of "historical imagination" through a series of steps that involve students in each of the phases of the writing process--prewriting, composing, and rewriting. Thus, the activity facilitates development of writing skills by providing a meaningful purpose or context, while helping students develop a sense of history that can then be built on throughout the year.

Objectives: At the conclusion of this activity, students will be better able to:

--form hypotheses about the function of an historical artifact

--express historical ideas through written work

Grade Level: 1-3

Materials and Preparation: The key material for this activity is an antique trunk stuffed with old-fashioned paraphernalia--books, bottles, pictures, fans, etc. For younger children, you may wish to heighten the atmosphere further by dressing in clothes of a bygone era and bringing additional "props" to class; these might include old chairs or "cobwebs" made from crepe paper streamers. A record about time, such as "Today, Yesterday, Tomorrow" (from the album Imagination and Me, Custom Records Production, St. Louis, Missouri), would also be helpful. You will also need copies of Handout 10 for all the students.

Adapted from "Exploring the Past: Writing About Real Stuff," by Kristin Smyka, in Writing in Elementary School Social Studies, edited by Barry K. Beyer and Robert Gilstrap (Social Science Education Consortium and ERIC Clearinghouse for Social Studies/Social Science Education, 1982), pp. 71-76. Used by permission. Poems by Laurel R. Singleton.

Procedure

1. Explain that today the class is going to think about a long time ago. You will do things to help students see, feel, hear, smell, and talk about a different way of living.

2. Ask each child to find a quiet, private place in the classroom. Turn the lights off and play a record of a song about time ("Today, Yesterday, Tomorrow" is excellent). Play the song twice so the children can listen to the lyrics. As an alternative, read one or both of the following poems about time.

YESTERDAY

Yesterday when I was small
I couldn't reach the cookie jar
Or turn the television on
Or walk too far
Without my mom.

I wore diapers
And pajamas with feet.
And didn't have much hair
Or many teeth.

It must have been fun.
Too bad I can't remember.

Now I'm older
And I can reach the cookie jar
So I have to help make them.
And I can turn on the TV
But I have to do my homework first.
I've got hair--and it hurts when
  Mom combs it.
And teeth just have to be brushed.

I wonder if I'll remember this when
  I am twelve.

MYSTERIES

Things that happened long ago
Are mysteries to me--
Why the cavemen wrote on walls.
What I did when I was three.

I wish I knew the answers
To the questions that I ask.
How fast could a covered wagon go?
Why did the witch doctor wear a mask?

What was the name of Paul Revere's horse?
Who invented the very first toy?
Why did Abe Lincoln grow a beard?
What was Dad like when he was a boy?

So many things have happened
Since the world began.
I want to know all about them
If I possibly can.

But the future has its mysteries too.
What will tomorrow hold?
Will I learn the mysteries of time
While I am growing old?

3. Regroup to discuss the notion of time, encouraging students to express their own conceptions. Role play some situations to help clarify simple time distinctions. For example, a student might dramatize play activities of "yesterday" as a two-year-old toddler, and "today" as a first-grade student. Help students distinguish between the past and current events, recognized as "now" or "today."

4. Point out the props you have brought to class, explaining that your classroom has been turned into an attic full of things from the past. Have the students pick partners. Each team can then come to the trunk and select an item. When all the teams have objects from the trunk, let the teams spend a few minutes sharing their ideas about how the items might have been used.

5. Again, reconvene as a large group and talk about how the children felt when they looked into the trunk or reached in to take an article. Ask questions about smell, sight, touch, and sound, developing a list of collectively descriptive words. Record these on a large sheet of paper visible to everyone. Words students have used in describing this phase of the activity have ranged from "squirmy," "tingly," and "breath-holding" to "icky," "yucky," and "aargh." Point out that some words describe people's feelings, while others identify smell, touch, or appearance.

6. Have the teams rejoin, with each pair choosing a place in the room where the partners can talk with one another. Pass out copies of Handout 10, and read the questions on the handout aloud. Let the students talk in their pairs, and then reassemble as a large group to share their hypotheses.

7. Tell students to find a place in the classroom where they can write privately and comfortably. Tell them to close their eyes and "make movies in their heads" as you talk through the simulated attic trip, cuing students with words from the group list. Remind the children of the hypotheses that were suggested during the group

discussion. Then ask the children to make up "movies" about their old objects and write them down.

8. Circulate to offer spelling assistance. When students have completed their work, do some stretching and deep breathing before they join their partners to exchange stories. Tell the students that they should each say one good thing about their partner's paper.

9. Form a large group. If some children wish to read their stories aloud, let them do so. To conclude the activity, replay the record or reread the poem.

Follow-up

Display a number of old pictures around the room. Individual students can select a person from a photograph and imagine that they are that person, writing about where they were when the photograph was taken. Groups of students can select a photograph and create a historical skit about the people shown: Why were they in the picture? What were their relationships? Encourage students to use "historical imagination" in creating lives for the photographed people.

WHAT AM I?

What do you think the object is?

When do you think it was made?

How do you think it was used?

Who do you think owned it?

Do you think this could be used today?

If so, in what manner?

Why was it in the trunk?

Who do you think put it in the trunk?

MY FOLKS CAME IN A COVERED WAGON

Overview

Elementary students are fascinated by stories of life on the frontier, but most of the information they have relates to events that involved adults. This activity provides students with the opportunity to learn about the lives of children on the frontier through the use of primary source material.

Objectives: At the conclusion of this activity, students will be better able to:

--list ways in which the lives of children on the frontier were similar to and different from the lives of modern children

--use primary source documents to obtain historical information

Grade Level: 4-6

Materials and Preparation: Make copies of Handout 11 for all the students.

Procedure

1. If the class has been studying life on the frontier, briefly review what they have learned about living conditions of the time. If the class has not been studying this period of U.S. history, briefly discuss with students what they know about early frontier life. Be sure students indicate the source of their information. Ask students to speculate about the lives of frontier children. What games did they play? Did they go to school? What did they eat?

2. Explain that one way to learn about the past is to read what people who lived then wrote. Tell students that they are going to read some stories written by people who were children on the frontier.

Activity by Laurel R. Singleton. Primary source material used in the handout adapted from My Folks Came in a Covered Wagon (Capper Publications, 1956), pp. 47-48, 64, 69. Used by permission of Stauffer Communications, Inc.

3. Distribute copies of the handout to all the students. Divide the class into five groups, assigning one of the handout passages to each group. Tell the groups to read and discuss their passages and then make two lists: one of ways in which the children described in the passage were like children of today and one of ways in which they were different. While the groups are working, provide any assistance needed in understanding unfamiliar vocabulary or sentence structure.

4. After about 15 minutes, have the class reconvene as a group. Each small group should share its passage and lists. Record the groups' lists on the chalkboard, combining them into master lists of differences and likenesses.

5. Conclude with a brief discussion of facets of childhood that appear to be constant and those that change from one time period to another.

Follow-up

Divide the class into small groups. Direct half of the groups to prepare skits depicting what would happen if two modern children (a boy and a girl) found themselves on the frontier. The remaining students should prepare skits illustrating what would happen if two pioneer children found themselves transported to your school. Provide time for students to present and discuss their skits.

As an alternative, have students interview parents, grandparents, or older friends and neighbors to find out more about aspects of childhood that change and/or remain the same over time.

Pig-a-Back Pioneers

We saw our first railroad when I came with my parents in a wagon train from Texas. There was whooping and cheering from the men and the boys--and all of us had to take a walk on the ties.

When we camped at night, the older children taught us little ones how to make shadow pictures on the tent walls. I was only three or four, but someone taught me to make a bunny rabbit. When we came to streams, the men and big boys would carry us small ones across on their backs to save the teams and because we thought it was fun. I have no idea how long we were on the road and there is no one left to ask.

I remember that when we reached our homestead, we ate off a wash tub turned upside down, and the grass around the place was so high that we children could hide from each other in it. Our first school was three miles away, and the men dragged a big log thru the tall grass to make a trail so we wouldn't get lost.

> Mrs. E. Mathis
> Custer City, Oklahoma

Tumbleweed Tree

When we lived in a two-room house--half dugout and half sod--on the Western Kansas prairie, we had no toys. We made our own amusements. We learned early to ride our ponies, and in the spring we gathered the lovely wild flowers.

Well do I remember our first Christmas tree. It was a tumbleweed decorated with paper chains and pictures taken from packages of Arbuckel coffee. My brothers learned to braid different colors of hair from the horses' tails to make attractive belts, quirts [whips], and bridles. Little sister spent much time holding the strands as her brothers braided.

The prairie was plentifully strewn [covered] with dried buffalo horns. We scraped and polished these to a lovely shining black and made coat and hat racks from them. We were happy. That fact stands out above all.

> Mrs. J.W. Edwards
> Meade, Kansas

Human Clothesline

It was a long, long trail a-winding that led us from Indiana to drouthy [dry] Kansas. There were nine of us, one a small baby--far too many to start so far in a covered wagon. It was a long, tiresome trip and it seemed to me it rained most of the time. We children slept under the wagon, and the rain would run under the wagon and get our beds wet.

With all the rain, there was no way to dry the "squares" for the baby. My sister and I had to be the clothesline and hold the diapers up before the campfire to dry them. We disliked this job very much. Some days we would make camp to get the washing done and let the horses rest.

I remember one blizzard after we got settled. We had plenty of fuel, but no water. We would open the door and dig out snow and melt it. One dry season the folks planted turnips and fall rains came in time for them to grow. We lived mostly on turnips that winter. I haven't cared for them since.

> Mrs. F. Modlin
> Burr Oak, Kansas

Cradle Lore

When I was nine years old, I remember hearing pioneer women tell about ways they saved time on busy days. One woman said she always put the big baby in one end of the cradle and the little baby in the other. As the big baby played, it kept jiggling the cradle and kept the little baby content.

Another neighbor said she put her baby in a high chair, put molasses on its fingers, and gave it a feather to play with. That kept it happy for hours. A third woman said she put her baby in the cradle and gave it a piece of fat meat to suck. She tied a string to the meat and attached the other end to the baby's toe. That way if the baby choked on the meat, it would start kicking and pull the meat out.

> Mrs. E. G. Caine
> Indianola, Nebraska

Father Made Furniture

My parents were married in 1876 and settled in midwestern Nebraska. They lived in a dugout near a small creek. They had a sod fireplace and a little stove for cooking. We burned cobs, cornstalks, sunflower stalks, and chips from the cow pasture.

Father made a table and other furniture that was very sturdy, but not very polished. One time we had two kegs for Father and Mother to sit on at the table. A man came by who wanted a keg for pickles, and he traded us a chair for one of the kegs. We children stood up at the table and didn't think anything about it because we were used to it.

Our parents didn't even have a table when they were first married. They sat on big pumpkins with the food spread out on a canvas on the bed. Once our lamp chimney got broken and Mother went to the smokehouse and got a saucer of lard. She buried a twisted cloth in the lard and lighted the end.

The first school my brother and I attended was in a neighbor's house. He had a two-room house and all the other homes had only one room. We had to furnish our own books and seats, so we had quite a variety. The teacher was a 17-year-old girl who was paid $15.00 per month.

We were 75 miles from a doctor. Mother had a toothache for several months and there was no relief for it until spring. She had to wait until her baby was born and a month old, and then we made the long trip to the dentist.

Jessie F. Gentry
Stratton, Colorado

SHOULD MEN HAVE THE VOTE?

Overview

This short activity can be used in a study of women's suffrage and the 19th Amendment. Its reverse sex stereotyping will provide an opportunity for lively class discussion.

Objectives: At the conclusion of this activity, students will be better able to:

--list implications of a power monopoly by one sex

--explain the meaning of equality under the law

Grade Level: 7-8

Materials and Preparation: You will need copies of Handout 12 for all the students. If you have not been studying women's suffrage, you might want to give students a brief description of the efforts that culminated in passage of the 19th Amendment before the activity.

Procedure

1. Distribute copies of Handout 12 and have students read Alice Miller's arguments.

2. Solicit student comments, asking such questions for discussion as:

--Why is Miller's argument so effective?

--Do you think sex stereotyping of women is as extreme as the sex stereotyping of men in Miller's argument? Do you think it was that extreme at the time women were working for passage of the 19th Amendment?

Adapted from Law in U.S. History: A Teacher Resource Manual, edited by Melinda R. Smith (New Mexico Law-Related Education Project, 1981), pp. 193-194. Used by permission of the New Mexico Law-Related Education Project, Box 25883, Albuquerque, NM 87125.

3.   Divide the class into groups of four or five students. Tell students to imagine a society in which women are the only persons allowed to vote, to hold political office, and to occupy positions of economic power. Have the small groups consider the following questions:

--Would everything be turned around, with men being discriminated against as women have been?

--Would things be pretty much the same as they are now?

--Some say present society is designed for the convenience of men. How would society look if it were designed for the convenience of women?

Follow-up

The women who fought for suffrage were a diverse group, ranging from left-wing radicals to upper class matrons. Many of the suffragists were involved in other political/social efforts. Encourage students to do research on such women as Susan B. Anthony, Carrie Chapman Catt, Anna Howard Shaw, Emma Goldman, Alva Vanderbilt Belmont, Mary McDowell, and Lucretia Mott. One interesting source is the correspondence of these women. After researching particular suffragists, students might write letters to them describing women's roles today.

WHY WE OPPOSE VOTES FOR MEN

1. BECAUSE MAN'S PLACE IS IN THE ARMY.

2. BECAUSE NO REALLY MANLY MAN WANTS TO SETTLE ANY
    QUESTION OTHERWISE THAN BY FIGHTING.

3. BECAUSE IF MEN SHOULD ADOPT PEACEABLE METHODS WOMEN
    WILL NO LONGER LOOK UP TO THEM.

4. BECAUSE MEN WILL LOSE THEIR CHARM IF THEY STEP OUT
    OF THEIR NATURAL SPHERE AND INTEREST THEMSELVES IN
    OTHER MATTERS THAN FEATS OF ARMS, UNIFORMS AND DRUMS.

5. BECAUSE MEN ARE TOO EMOTIONAL TO VOTE. THEIR CONDUCT
    AT BASEBALL GAMES AND POLITICAL CONVENTIONS SHOWS THIS
    WHILE THEIR INNATE TENDENCY TO APPEAL TO FORCE RENDERS
    THEM PARTICULARLY UNFIT FOR THE TASK OF GOVERNMENT.

                        Alice Duer Miller, 1915

WHAT WOULD YOU PACK?

Overview

In this small-group activity, students list in order of priority what things they would have brought with them if they had immigrated to the United States from Europe during the late 1800s. The discussion following the exercise helps students recognize how great a change occurred in the lives of immigrants upon their arrival in this country.

Objectives: At the conclusion of this activity, students will be better able to:

--recognize that an individual brought up in one culture and then thrust into contact with another faces serious problems of adjustment

--form tentative hypotheses about what aspects of immigrants' behavior are likely to change most rapidly and which are likely to be most resistant to change

Grade Level: 5-8

Materials and Preparation: You will need to make copies of Handout 13 for use by small groups of students. Cut apart the cards on the handout prior to the activity. You will also need several large sheets of posting paper or wrapping paper.

Procedure

1. Divide the class into groups of four or five students. Each group will receive a copy of the handout, which shows 27 things which immigrants might have brought with them to this country. Explain to students that each group will pretend that it is a family immigrating to the United States in the late 1800s. Because of weight and space

Adapted from "What Would You Pack?," by Bruce E. Tipple and Pamela Whitehead, in Ethnic Studies Sampler: The Best of the Title IX Project Materials, edited by Frances Haley (Social Science Education Consortium and ERIC Clearinghouse for Social Studies/Social Science Education, 1981), pp. 261-262. Used by permission.

restrictions, they--like other immigrants--will not be able to bring a great many belongings with them to the new land. Usually, immigrant families brought one trunk full of belongings. They were also required to bring a food pack for the long voyage. Sometimes, a family would bring a favorite piece of furniture.

2. Now explain to each group that their food pack may include such things as smoked meat, salted fish, bread, cheese, canned honey, and water. Each group should decide on ten items they would have packed in their trunk. They should place the cards for these items in order of importance on a sheet of posting or wrapping paper. For each item, an explanation of why it was chosen should also be written on the paper.

3. Each group should then decide on one additional item to be taken to the new world: a musical instrument, a piece of furniture, or a spinning wheel. The card picturing the item chosen should be placed on the paper with reasons for its selection.

4. The sheets from the groups should be taped to the classroom walls or hung on the bulletin board. Each group should briefly explain their selections.

5. Hold a brief class discussion to summarize the activity. The following questions will help guide the discussion:

--Were there some things you wanted to bring but had to leave behind? If so, what were they?

--Do you think the immigrants had to leave some things behind? How do you think they felt about leaving those things behind?

--When the immigrants arrived here, what kinds of things did they need? Why?

--What kinds of things could the immigrants continue to do as they had done in the old country? Why?

--What kinds of changes would they have to make? Why?

Follow-up

Invite a recent immigrant to the United States to speak to your class about the process of entering this country. Was he/she able to bring unlimited personal belongings to this country? How did the lack or availability of one's belongings affect the adjustment process?

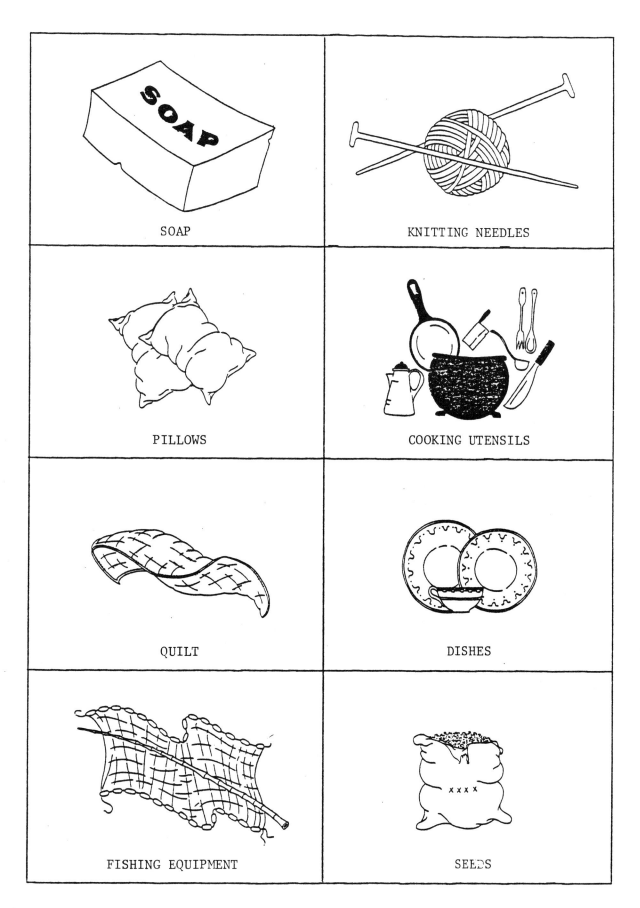

SOAP

KNITTING NEEDLES

PILLOWS

COOKING UTENSILS

QUILT

DISHES

FISHING EQUIPMENT

SEEDS

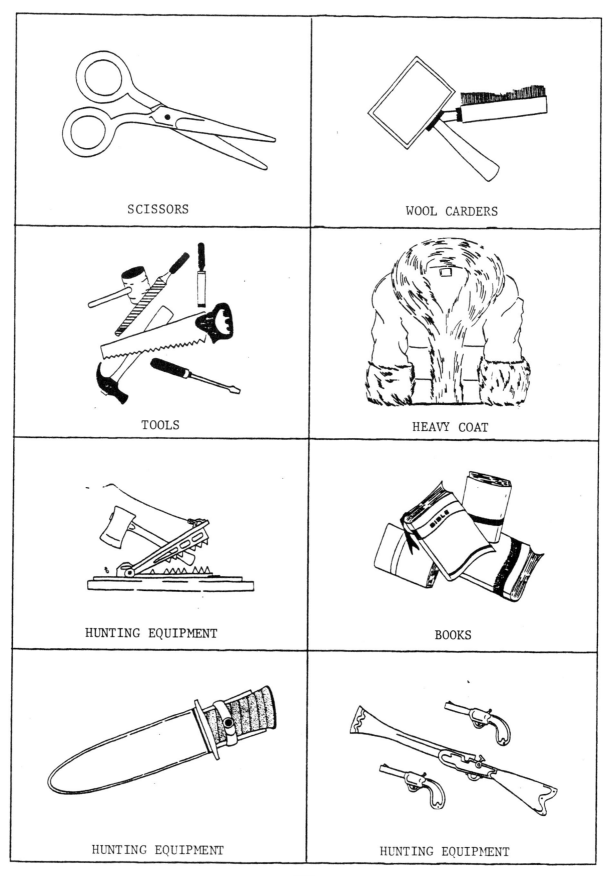

SCISSORS

WOOL CARDERS

TOOLS

HEAVY COAT

HUNTING EQUIPMENT

BOOKS

HUNTING EQUIPMENT

HUNTING EQUIPMENT

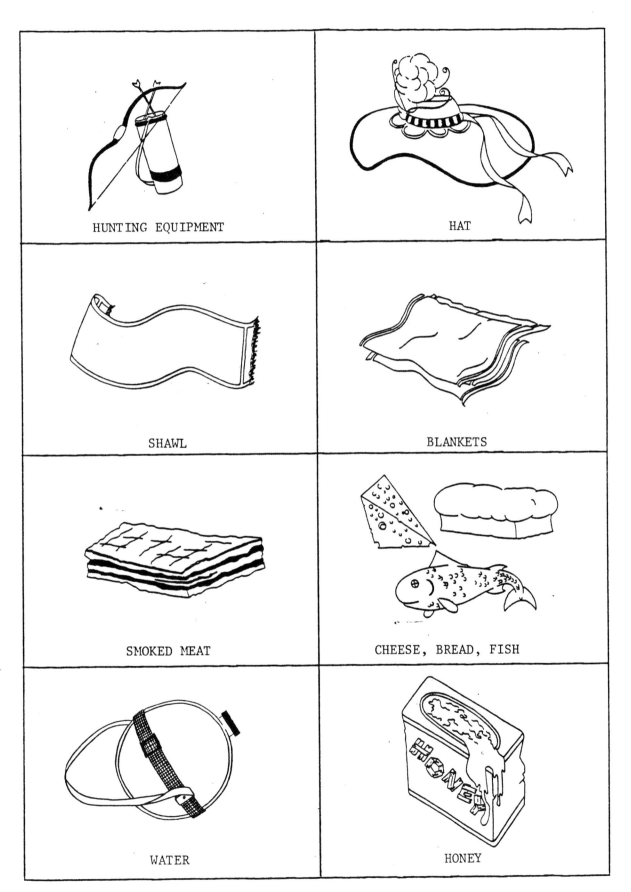

HUNTING EQUIPMENT

HAT

SHAWL

BLANKETS

SMOKED MEAT

CHEESE, BREAD, FISH

WATER

HONEY

SPINNING WHEEL

FURNITURE

MUSICAL INSTRUMENTS

THE LAND OF MILK AND HONEY

Overview

Imagine a class of students curiously eyeing honey graham crackers and milk cartons resting on a table across the room, with only a couple of tables separating the students from the goodies. Imagine also the reactions when, at the conclusion of this activity, only some of the class members are entitled to share in this "Land of Milk and Honey," with the rest standing empty-handed. Imagine further how these same students will feel when they realize that they are re-creating a scene possibly played out by their ancestors when the latter sought to enjoy the beneficence of that promised land, America.

Those are the experiences students will have in this simulation, which is fun, stimulating, and easy to use. It attempts to fit the discovery mode using hypothetical or actual data; yet it is heuristic in that it encourages students to look beyond the immediacy of the simulation, the text, or the specific course content and context.

Objectives: At the conclusion of this activity, students will be better able to:

--list problems associated with entry into this country

--develop hypotheses as to why the system was this way

--propose a plan that would make the quota system fair to all

Grade Level: 7-8

Materials and Preparation: You will need copies of Handout 14 for all the students, two copies of Handout 15, and one set of the data

---

Adapted from "The Land of Milk and Honey," by Wayne Mahood, in "Classroom Teacher's 'Idea' Notebook," Social Education 44, no. 1 (January 1980), pp. 22-24. Used by permission of the National Council for the Social Studies and Wayne Mahood.

cards reproduced on five colors of paper. You will also need two large tables, one smaller table, and a supply of graham crackers and milk. If students have not been studying immigration, you may wish to read them a textbook selection on immigration in the early 1900s before the activity.

Procedure

1. As students enter the classroom at the beginning of the class period, tell them they are immigrants. Give two students copies of Handout 15, explaining that they will be "doctors" and directing them to set up examining stations at the two small tables. Give the remaining students copies of Handout 14, have each draw a data card from a bag or box, and ask them to proceed directly to the front chalkboard. No talking will be allowed.

2. Have the students read their data cards and instruction sheets and then line up to approach the doctors' tables.

3. The "doctors" should process the immigrants, deciding on the basis of their quotas whether individual immigrants will be allowed to enter the "Land of Milk and Honey."

4. Students who are not allowed to enter should return to their desks. Those who are allowed to enter should go through a second phase of processing, in which you administer "literacy tests." Students who are finally accepted for entry can proceed to the "Land of Milk and Honey," taking a portion of graham crackers and milk.

5. When all students have been processed, all should return to their desks. Distribute crackers and milk to all the students.

6. Debrief the simulation by discussing such questions as the following:

--How did you feel standing in line awaiting your turn? After you were admitted? After you were rejected?

--What problems did you encounter as you sought entry?

--What reasons might be offered for admittance? rejection?

--Did you feel discriminated against? Was there any prejudice shown?

--What led you to believe there were some qualifications or limits on the number admitted?

--What were the qualifications of those admitted? Rejected?

--Was there a pattern to the acceptances or rejections? If so, how would you describe this pattern?

--Would this pattern have existed throughout the history of the United States?

--Why might patterns exist? What effects might they have on the United States? On the countries against which discrimination was shown? Economically? Socially? Politically?

--Given the chance, in what ways would you revise the admissions plan?

--What effects might your plan have?

--Having done this simulation, what conclusions can you draw about the immigrant experience?

Follow-up

Based on experience with this lesson, the preceding questions could lead to discussion extending well into another class period or two and could lead to examination of the effects on American society of quotas in terms of the economy, social life, and politics. This, in turn, could lead to discussion of the nature of the discredited melting pot theory. Associated concepts stemming from this simulation and discussion are assimilation, accommodation, culture, social change, social classes, and freedom and equality. Further discussions could draw comparisons with other time periods in the United States; with other countries which have experienced significant numbers of immigrants, including those asked to admit Vietnamese exiles; or with countries that have colonized North America and their policies for assimilation and accommodation.

INSTRUCTIONS TO STUDENTS
(IMMIGRANTS)

You have just been given a "visa" (data card) to America and must remain on the ship (at the chalkboard) until you have finished reading this page. When you have, take your visa and line up single file in front of one of the doctor's tables. There will be two lines. You have disembarked from the ship and are now waiting to enter the United States. There are several different colored visas:

Green	(Irish)
Blue	(German)
Red	(Slavic)
White	(English)
Yellow	(Italian)

The doctors have instructions as to entry. They determine who will be permitted entry to the "Land of Milk and Honey"--the United States. Please hand your visa to the doctor as you approach the table for your examination. The doctors will return your visa, and, if admitted, you will present it to the "literacy officer" at the third table.

If you speak English, depending on the country of origin, you may be able to "bargain" with the doctors or literacy officer. Otherwise, whatever you say will be disregarded.

Remember--your objective is to get into the "Land of Milk and Honey," but there are certain qualifications you must meet and regulations you must follow, including remaining in line until your turn.

INSTRUCTIONS TO DOCTORS

You are one of the two doctors who are to examine the immigrants as they come into America. The specific quota you must follow is:

5	Green	(Irish)
8	Blue	(German)
3	Red	(Slavic)
10	White	(English)
4	Yellow	(Italian)

This is the total number of each nationality that you may admit into the United States. Keep in mind that WASPS (White Anglo-Saxon Protestants) are preferred, but other factors such as vocational skills, literacy, health, and religion are also to be considered. Few persons are purely WASP, literate, and in good health. You and the other doctor can discuss whom you will admit.

Number of applicants:

6	Green	(Irish)
7	Blue	(German)
5	Red	(Slavic)
4	White	(English)
6	Yellow	(Italian)

VISA Age: 60 Skilled, illiterate Typhoid Male Roman Catholic Irish	VISA Age: 12 Unskilled, literate Malnourished Female Protestant Irish
VISA Age: 57 Skilled, literate Poor health Female Roman Catholic Irish	VISA Age: 45 Unskilled, literate Good health Male Roman Catholic Irish
VISA Age: 32 Unskilled, illiterate Good health Male Roman Catholic Irish	VISA Age: 19 Skilled, illiterate Tuberculosis Female Roman Catholic Irish

VISA	VISA
Age: 68 Skilled, literate Poor health Male Protestant German	Age: 5 Unskilled, illiterate Good health Female Protestant German
VISA	VISA
Age: 15 Unskilled, illiterate Good health Female Protestant German	Age: 40 Skilled, literate Poor health Male Protestant German
VISA	VISA
Age: 55 Skilled, literate Good health Male Jewish German	Age: 37 Skilled, illiterate Poor health Male Protestant German
VISA	
Age: 25 Unskilled, literate Good health Female Jewish German	

VISA

Age: 7
Unskilled, illiterate
Good health
Female
Roman Catholic
Slavic

VISA

Age: 29
Skilled, illiterate
Poor health
Female
Roman Catholic
Slavic

VISA

Age: 57
Skilled, literate
Poor health
Male
Jewish
Slavic

VISA

Age: 45
Unskilled, illiterate
Good health
Male
Protestant
Slavic

VISA

Age: 33
Skilled, illiterate
Poor health
Male
Roman Catholic
Slavic

VISA Age: 35 Unskilled, illiterate Good health Male Anglican English	VISA Age: 25 Skilled, literate Good health Female Anglican English
VISA Age: 65 Skilled, illiterate Poor health Male Protestant English	VISA Age: 15 Unskilled, literate . Poor health Female Protestant English

VISA	VISA
Age: 68 Skilled, illiterate Poor health Female Roman Catholic Italian	Age: 45 Skilled, literate Poor health Male Roman Catholic Italian
VISA	VISA
Age: 37 Skilled, illiterate Good health Female Roman Catholic Italian	Age: 17 Unskilled, illiterate Good health Male Roman Catholic Italian
VISA	VISA
Age: 25 Skilled, literate Good health Female Jewish Italian	Age: 10 Unskilled, illiterate Good health Male Roman Catholic Italian

Section 6

UNDERSTANDING THE WORLD

The first three activities in this section focus on global "connectedness." The first activity, "The Pebble in the Pond," demonstrates for students how one event may have a range of possible effects. In the second activity, "Global Connections," students examine how members of their class are connected to the rest of the world. "Match a Proverb and Find Its Home," the third activity, involves students in a game that indicates similarities in folk wisdom around the world. The remaining activities in the section focus on specific global issues or problems: human rights, resource distribution, and conflict resolution.

THE PEBBLE IN THE POND

Overview

   We let many events occur in our lives and in the world without giving much thought to the repercussions they may have. An awareness of the myriad possible effects of events may better prepare students to anticipate and respond appropriately to them.

Objectives: At the conclusion of this activity, students will be better able to:
   --imagine possible effects of a stated cause
   --logically think about causes and effects
   --understand how events can affect people directly and indirectly

Grade Level: 1-4

Materials and Preparation: You will need to gather the following materials: pieces of sponge or styrofoam or ping pong balls, a large pail or tub, a pebble, butcher paper, colored posterboard, and crayons, markers, pens, and/or pencils. You will also need to make copies of Handout 16 for all the students.

Procedure

   1. Fill the tub or pail with water. Ask students what they think will happen to the water if you drop a pebble into it. Demonstrate the rippling effect by dropping the pebble into the water. Be sure students observe the wave motion. Now place two ping pong balls (or pieces of sponge or styrofoam) on the water, one close to the center where the pebble is dropped and one farther away. Ask students which ball will be moved when the pebble is dropped. Do the same thing with five or more

Reprinted with permission from the Center for Teaching International Relations (CTIR), University of Denver. Adapted from Teaching About Global Awareness: An Approach for Grades 1-6, by Junelle Barrett and others, pp. 11-12, 107. Copyright 1981, CTIR.

balls. Tell the students to watch the balls carefully when you drop the pebble. (All of the balls should be affected by the pebble, regardless of their placement on the water.)

2. Challenge students to find a place on the water where a ball will not be moved by the pebble. Have students put their names on balls and place them in the tub. Which balls will be affected by the pebble? Drop the pebble, reminding students to pay close attention to what happens. Discuss:

--Which balls were affected the most? The least?

--Were any balls not affected at all?

--Name happenings or events that might have the same effect as dropping the pebble (a decision, an argument, a kind word, a spit ball, a joke). Help students understand that events can have the same effect as the pebble and its splash--even though we are not nearby, one of the growing circles might touch us.

3. Distribute Handout 16 to illustrate how the ripple effect can work. Ask students if they can draw more circles on the model to represent other effects or changes that might occur or other people who might be affected by the new rule.

4. Pick an event that is fresh in students' minds and is obviously affecting their lives (e.g., a new teacher or principal, special assembly, unusual weather, or vacation). Have the class brainstorm a list of things that might logically happen because of that event. Remind them that positive and negative effects can occur. Also encourage students to consider the effects the event might have on their own lives. As a group, draw on the chalkboard a ripple effect model showing the event's repercussions.

5. Divide the class into four or five groups. Have the groups choose another event that would start a ripple effect and construct a model. The models can be constructed by cutting posterboard into circles and pasting them on butcher paper to represent the event and its effects. The events, effects, and dotted lines connecting the two can be drawn with crayons, marking pens, pens, or pencils. After students have written all the effects they can think of, they can draw the circular ripples to connect the sequence.

Follow-up

The ripple effects model is similar to the futures wheel, which can be introduced to older students in a follow-up activity. In making a futures wheel (see example below), students should write an event in the center of a piece of paper or the chalkboard, draw a circle around it, and draw a number of lines extending from the circle. At the end of each line, they should write something that might occur as a result of the event and circle these results. The process is then continued for each of the new circles. In Creating Futures Activity Cards (Minneapolis Public Schools, 1979), Elizabeth Klenzman and Paula Taylor suggest making futures wheels for such topics as using more solar energy, discovery of intelligent life in space, inflation of gasoline prices to $10.00 per gallon, linkage of human brains with computers, and development of medical techniques that allow people to live to the age of 800.

FUTURES WHEEL

RIPPLES

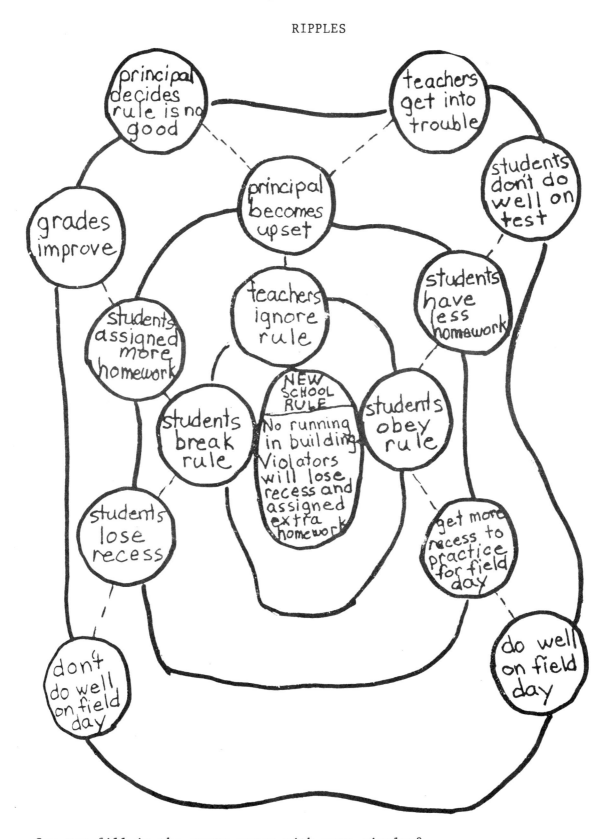

Can you fill in the empty space with more circles?

GLOBAL CONNECTIONS

Overview

In this activity, students discover how their class is connected to the rest of the world. Using a bingo-game format, students look for classmates who fit appropriate squares on their game sheets. Each square represents a certain kind of "global connection."

Objectives: At the conclusion of this activity, students will be better able to:

--explain how members of their class are connected to other parts of the world

    --list some reasons why these connections exist

    --speculate about further "global connections"

Grade Level: 3-8

Materials and Preparation: Prepare copies of Handout 17 for all the students. Be sure a large world map and push pins are available.

Procedure

1. Distribute copies of Handout 17. Explain that the object of "Globingo" is to fill in as many squares as possible with the names of classmates who fit those squares. When one row--horizontal, vertical, or diagonal--has been completely filled in, the student has scored a "globingo." (Note: You may want to award prizes or points to the first students who score.) Point out that the code key on the handout explains the letter-coded spaces on the game sheet. Emphasize that the name of the relevant country, as well as the student's name, should be recorded in each square. Explain that each student may sign another classmate's sheet only once, even if more than one square could apply to that student. (This rule encourages maximum interaction.)

From Global Issues in the Intermediate Classroom: Grades 5-8, by Jacquelyn Johnson and John Benegar (Social Science Education Consortium and ERIC Clearinghouse for Social Studies/Social Science Education, 1981), pp. 5-7. Used by permission.

2. Allow 10-15 minutes for students to walk around the classroom looking for classmates who fit the various squares. It is important during this interaction period that students actively ask questions of one another rather than passively handing around the game sheets. Students should continue to try to fill up their game sheets even after they have scored one or more "globingos." Try to keep the game going until every student has scored.

3. You might want to let the students continue to fill in their squares during recess or the lunch period in order to collect the maximum amount of information. Students might also enjoy involving their families and other adults in this activity. In this case, you will need to postpone the debriefing until a subsequent class period.

4. Ask students what they learned about one another in the process of filling in their "globingo" squares. What was the most surprising thing they learned about any of their classmates?

5. On a large map of the world, help students locate all the nations identified in this activity by cutting apart the squares on the game sheets and pinning them to the appropriate locations on a world map. Are students surprised at all these "connections" their class has with the rest of the world? What would the map look like if game sheets from another class were included? Would students discover more connections? What if the entire school participated in this activity?

6. Probe students to explain the reasons for all the connections they found in this activity. What caused these connections? In what ways do we learn more about the rest of the world? Television? Travel? Newspapers? Trading among nations?

7. Ask students what they think the phrase "shrinking world" means. Do the processes listed previously contribute to a "shrinking world"? In what ways? Do students think they will become more "connected" to the rest of the world in the future? In what ways?

Follow-up

To help students assess global interdependence on a personal level, ask them to think of other ways in which they and their families are connected to the rest of the world. Some students might enjoy using these new ideas to develop another game sheet for their class.

GLOBINGO

Find someone who:

A. has traveled to some foreign country

B. has a pen pal in another country

C. is learning a foreign language

D. has a relative in another country

E. has helped a visitor from another country

F. enjoys a music group from another country

G. is wearing something that was made in another country

H. enjoys eating foods from other countries

I. can name a famous sports star from another country

J. has a family car that was made in another country

K. has talked to someone who has lived in another country

L. lives in a home where more than one language is spoken

M. saw a story about another country in the newspaper recently

N. learned something about another country on TV recently

O. owns a TV or other appliance made in another country

P. has a parent or other relative who was born in another country

A	B	C	D
_____ name	_____ name	_____ name	_____ name
_____ country	_____ country	_____ country	_____ country
E	F	G	H
_____ name	_____ name	_____ name	_____ name
_____ country	_____ country	_____ country	_____ country
I	J	K	L
_____ name	_____ name	_____ name	_____ name
_____ country	_____ country	_____ country	_____ country
M	N	O	P
_____ name	_____ name	_____ name	_____ name
_____ country	_____ country	_____ country	_____ country

MATCH A PROVERB AND FIND ITS HOME

Overview

The folk wisdom of countries around the world reveals many of the commonalities shared by people regardless of the cultures in which they live. This activity, presented as a game, provides students with an opportunity to examine proverbs from many nations. Practice in working with a world map is also provided.

Objectives: At the conclusion of this activity, students will be better able to:

--understand that people around the world have much in common

--cite proverbs from other cultures that reflect the same values embodied in American proverbs

Grade Level: 5-8

Materials and Preparation: A large world map is needed for this game.

Procedure

1. Choose two students to serve as judges for the game. One will decide how well proverbs "match," awarding from one to three points on the basis of that decision. The other will judge whether the proverb's land of origin is located correctly on a world map; three points will be awarded if the location is pinpointed correctly and promptly, one or two points will be awarded if the location is found after some hesitation or if the general vicinity is correct but the specific location is incorrect.

Adapted from "Folk Wit and Wisdom," by Judith M. Barnet, Intercom 90/91: Culture's Storehouse: Building Humanities Skills Through Folklore, pp. 17-18. Copyright 1978 by Global Perspectives in Education, 218 East 18th Street, New York, NY 10003. Used by permission.

2.   Select one student to serve as the "reader." The reader will read aloud--one by one--the proverbs listed below. The reader should announce the country or continent of origin for each proverb as it is read.

3.   Those students who are not judges or the reader should be divided into two teams, A and B. First a student on team A should try to "match" the proverb read by supplying another of comparable meaning and should indicate on a world map the country or continent of the first proverb's origin. If the person on team A is unsuccessful, then a member of team B gets a try, and so on. For example, the reader might recite the following: "Palm nuts do not ripen while you stand under a tree--a proverb from Africa." The student on team A might respond with this "matching" proverb: "A watched pot never boils." The contestant would then go to the world map and use a pointer or ruler to identify Africa. The team which amasses the largest number of points is the winner.

Proverbs and Their Lands of Origin

1.   Chickens always come home to roost. (Alabama)
2.   Ice three feet thick isn't frozen in a day. (China)
3.   Young gambler--old beggar. (Germany)
4.   Where the river is deepest, it makes the least noise. (Italy)
5.   If you climb up a tree, you must climb down that same tree. (Ghana)
6.   You cannot get two skins from one cow. (England)
7.   Eggs must not quarrel with stones. (China)
8.   A horse that arrives early gets good drinking water. (Africa)
9.   The love of money is the root of all evil. (Israel)
10.   Words thoughtlessly said cannot be called back. (Louisiana)
11.   The wife at another's house has the pretty eyes. (Africa)
12.   God gives the milk but not the pail. (Germany)
13.   Punch yourself to know how painful it is to others. (Japan)
14.   A bird in the hand is worth a hundred flying. (Mexico)
15.   Sing and cares disappear. (Poland)
16.   One man's story is not story; hear both sides. (Japan)
17.   God is a good worker, but he loves to be helped. (Spain)
18.   Many a good man is to be found under a shabby hat. (China)
19.   Fine clothes don't make the man. (Japan)

20. By trying often, the monkey learns to jump from the tree. (Zaire)
21. You can force a man to shut his eyes, but you can't make him sleep. (Denmark)
22. Two captains sink the ship. (Japan)
23. Little by little grow the bananas. (Benin, formerly Dahomey)
24. If you want to go fast, go the old road. (Burma)
25. Six feet of earth makes all men equal. (Italy)
26. Eat to live, not live to eat. (Greece)
27. He who stands with his feet on two ships will be drowned. (Russia, now the USSR)
28. A little in your own pocket is better than much in another's purse. (Spain)
29. Joy, moderation, and rest shut out the doctors. (Germany)
30. He who rides the tiger finds it difficult to dismount. (China)

Follow-up

A great deal of wisdom lies in all the proverbs gathered in this lesson. Ask students to pick the five proverbs they consider to be especially wise. Have students write papers pointing out what is to be learned from these proverbs. Could they serve as the broad outline for a philosophy of life? As an alternative, have students write papers explaining why the five proverbs selected are their favorites. What can they learn about themselves from their selections? Could each student's selections become a broad outline for his or her autobiography? Ask students to share and discuss their papers with the class.

HUMAN RIGHTS

Overview

In this activity, students examine the implications of particular rights by developing lists of rights they believe will create an atmosphere of respect and consideration in the classroom. They then compare their "declarations" with the United Nations Declaration of Children's Rights.

Objectives: At the conclusion of this activity, students will be better able to:

--define a human right

--list human rights, particularly children's rights

--explain why different groups confer different rights

--participate in group decision-making processes

Grade Level: 5-8

Materials and Preparation: Make copies of Handout 18 for the students.

Procedure

1. Discuss with students the meaning of the term "rights." (A right is a power or privilege to which someone is entitled.) Do children have rights? (Yes.) Do people have the same rights in every setting? Do children? (No. Children might have different rights at home, at school, and while riding their bicycles on the street. They would have different rights if they lived in another country.) Why do rights differ from group to group? (Because the groups have different values and purposes for granting rights.)

This activity is based on an idea suggested in The Cultural Exchange: A Cross-Cultural and Interdisciplinary Multicultural Education Curriculum for Grades 4-8, by Mary Nethery and others (Humboldt Co. Office of Education, Eureka, California, 1980).

2. Explain that one of your purposes is to create an atmosphere of respect and consideration in your classroom. What rights--for student and teacher--would be necessary to create such an atmosphere? Have students brainstorm a list of rights, ensuring that they follow the rules of brainstorming:

--Say anything that comes to mind.

--Piggybacking on the ideas of others is good.

--Don't evaluate or criticize what others say.

--When you can't think of anything, wait a minute and try again.

3. Divide the class into groups of four or five students, explaining that each group is going to develop a "Declaration of Student/Teacher Rights" for your class. Have each group consider the list generated in step 2, discussing each idea and adding to or deleting from the list. When all group members feel comfortable with the ideas, have students write them in the form of a declaration and have each group member sign the list. To help students in the drafting of their declarations, you might want to write several sample rights statements on the chalkboard while the groups are working.

4. Reconvene the class and have each group present its declaration. Note differences among the groups, pointing out, when possible, the values that the differences reflect.

5. Distribute copies of Handout 18, explaining that it is a declaration of children's rights developed by the United Nations to apply to all children around the world. Ask students what the declaration tells them about the nations of the world. Do all children have these rights in practice?

Follow-up

Encourage interested children to research the Universal Declaration of Human Rights and report to the class on how it differs from the Declaration of Children's Rights. Another topic for research by older students might be violations of human rights and the U.S. government's attitude regarding such violations. Students might debate whether human rights violations by the government of another country should take precedence over other considerations in determining whether the United States maintains normal relations with that country.

CHILDREN'S RIGHTS

1. The child shall enjoy the rights stated in this Declaration.

2. The child shall enjoy special protection by law.

3. The child has a right to have a name and to be a member of a country.

4. The child has the right to grow and be healthy. The child has the right to good food, housing, and health services.

5. The child who is disabled shall be given special treatment and care.

6. The child needs love and understanding.

7. The child has the right to go to school. The child shall have exercise, fun, and play.

8. The child shall be among the first to receive protection and help.

9. The child shall not be hired for work until of proper age.

WORLD FOOD SUPPLY

Overview

This lesson uses a simple simulation to examine four important concepts: population, hunger, needs, and wants. While the activity is an oversimplification of the problems of resource distribution, it will stimulate students to think about this critical problem.

Objectives: At the conclusion of this lesson, students will be better able to:

--explain how the world's food supply is distributed

--understand that not all people in the world get enough to eat

--express their opinions about the distribution of the world's food supply

--identify needs and wants of some people in the world

Grade Level: 3-6

Materials and Preparation: Obtain one piece of candy for each student. Post a large map of the world in your classroom.

Procedure

1. Tell students that you are going to turn the classroom into a mini-model of the world. Use a wall map of the world and move desks and chairs together to coincide with the land representations on the map. Then ask students to "move" to one of the continents, dividing the class in proportion with the world's population. For example, in a class of 32, the following number of students should be assigned to each continent: North America--2; Europe--4; Asia--20; Latin America--3; Africa--3; Australia--0. Point out that people do live in Australia,

---

Adapted from There's More than the Three R's to Those Early Years, by Dorothy J. Skeel and Ronald E. Sterling, paper presented at the annual meeting of the National Council for the Social Studies, November 1978. Used by permission of the authors.

but the number is so small, it would have to be represented by one-fifth of a student.

2. Inform the students that you are now going to divide all the food in the world among them. From your bag of candy, representing food, pass out the following number of pieces of candy to each "continent": North America, 14; Europe, 4; Asia, 5; Latin America, 3; Africa, 3; Australia, 1.

3. Allow students to react to their particular situation. Ask the students in Asia: How do you feel? How will you divide your food supply? Will some get more than others? What do you think about the group in North America? Get similar reactions from the groups in Africa and Latin America. Then ask the North American group how they feel. How will they divide their food supply? Will some get more than others? Are there some families in the United States that have more food than other families? How do you feel about the South Americans who do not have enough food to go around? How do you think the world can solve this problem? Why don't they solve this problem easily?

4. Point out that this is an oversimplification of the problem of maldistribution of resources and that not all people in Asia, Africa, and South America are starving and at the same time not all people in North America have enough food. Allow students to work out a redistribution of their "food supply."

Follow-up

Create a bulletin board display about the activities of UNICEF, which is one of the agencies that redistributes resources with special emphasis on the needs of children. Many materials about UNICEF are available from the U.S. Committee for UNICEF, 331 East 38th Street, New York, NY 10016.

GRAB THE BANANAS

Overview

This simulation game, adapted from the famous <u>Prisoners' Dilemma</u>, involves pairs of students in a simulated conflict situation in which they can either choose to cooperate or act aggressively. A thorough debriefing or postgame discussion is crucial if effective learning is to occur.

<u>Objectives</u>: At the conclusion of this activity, students will be better able to:

--list factors which contribute to escalating aggression between conflicting parties

--list factors which contribute to increasing cooperation between conflicting parties

--describe some of the costs and benefits of cooperating and acting aggressively in a conflict situation

<u>Grade Level</u>: 6-8

<u>Materials and Preparation</u>: Draw the matrix below on the chalkboard:

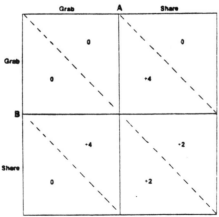

Adapted from "Grab the Bananas: A Simple Example of a Simulation Game," by William A. Nesbitt, <u>Intercom 75: Teaching Global Issues Through Simulations: It Can Be Easy</u>, pp. 4-5. Copyright 1974 by Global Perspectives in Education, 218 East 18th Street, New York, NY 10003. Used by permission.

Procedure

1. Divide the class into groups of three, with one person in each group designated as player A, one as player B, and the third as referee-scorekeeper. The players should sit across from each other with a desk or table in between; the referee should sit at the side.

2. Read the following explanation to the players: A and B are the sole survivors of a shipwreck and have managed to reach, in a weakened condition, a remote desert island. You come from different countries and cannot communicate verbally with each other because of the language barrier. Rescue is uncertain, but in any event will not occur before ten days. The island contains one source of food--bananas; given your condition, you can harvest only four a day. There is a chance that this may not be enough for both of you to survive. You have two choices--you can share the four bananas (two apiece), or you can try to grab all four.

3. Explain the results of their choices to the players, using the matrix you have drawn on the chalkboard. Note that if both players grab, they will lose the bananas through their destruction. If one grabs and the other shares, the assumption is that the person sharing has a trusting attitude and, in effect, turns his back on the other, who successfully grabs all four bananas.

4. To begin play, the referee for each group will say, "1, 2, 3, show!" whereupon each player will bring his/her hand up from under the desk or table with either an open palm (sharing) or a closed fist (grabbing). The referee will conduct ten rounds, one for each day on the island, and will mark the score on a piece of paper on which there are two columns, one labeled A and one B.

5. After all the teams have finished their rounds, begin the debriefing by raising questions about what happened. (The scores of each pair might be put on the chalkboard.) Did grabbing by one party early in the rounds lead to mistrust and set up an escalation of grabbing? Did those who cooperated generally have a better chance of survival? Did individuals attempt to use some strategy; for example, cooperating at the beginning and lulling the other person into thinking that cooperation would prevail? Did such a strategy work?

6. Discuss to what extent the game was realistic. How might they have been able to communicate? Would real people in such a situation behave as students did in the game? Would they have been more or less cooperative? Is it realistic that only one source of food was available?

7. Were any value questions involved in playing the game? If students who believe in sharing as a matter of principle grabbed in the game, why did they do this?

8. How might the game be changed to make it more realistic? What if the outcomes of action choices were changed? For example, what if the penalty for both parties' grabbing was increased each time it occurred to indicate not only the loss of the bananas but also greater violence between the two? Thus, the first time both grabbed, they would receive 0 each, -2 the next time, -4 the third, etc. Perhaps when they reached -8, it might be said that both parties were dead. How would such changes of the values on the matrix affect the action choices? Discuss the question of cost/benefits in making decisions; that is, if we have a clear idea of the eventual cost of certain decisions in relation to benefits, we might behave quite differently.

9. Have students consider what would happen if the scenario were changed so that the two parties saw themselves as enemies from the beginning; for example, one a Russian and the other a Chinese. What if both parties were friends, or husband and wife who loved each other deeply? What if the game were played with Bushmen or on an Israeli kibbutz? (If students know something about these cultures, they may hypothesize a more cooperative spirit.) Are Americans apt to grab?

Follow-up

Have interested students use the basic matrix to design their own games and try them out on each other. They might consider ways that the game could represent not just two people but two nations. One such scenario is provided in #5 of the NCSS "Teaching Social Studies in an Age of Crisis" series, Teaching Youth about Conflict and War (pp. 79-83). In that version, the USSR and U.S. are the parties in a dispute over the ownership of the islands in the Bering Sea on which oil has been discovered.

REFERENCES

Sources of all the activities in this book are described in this annotated bibliography. Most of the references have been entered into the ERIC (Educational Resources Information Center) system. Each is identified by a six-digit number and two letters: "EJ" for journal articles, "ED" for other documents. Abstracts of and descriptive information about all ERIC documents are published in two cumulative indexes: Resources in Education (RIE) for ED listings and the Current Index to Journals in Education (CIJE) for EJ listings. This information is also accessible through three major on-line computer searching systems: DIALOG, ORBIT, and BRS.

Most, but not all, ERIC documents are available for viewing in microfiche (MF) at libraries that subscribe to the ERIC collection. Microfiche copies of these documents can also be purchased from the ERIC Document Reproduction Service (EDRS), Box 190, Arlington, VA 22210. Paper copies of some documents can also be purchased from EDRS. Complete price information is provided in this bibliography. When ordering from EDRS, be sure to list the ED number, specify either MF or PC, and enclose a check or money order. Add postage to the MF or PC price at the rate of $1.55 for up to 75 microfiche or paper copy pages. Add $0.39 for each additional 75 microfiche or pages. One microfiche contains up to 96 document pages.

Journal articles are not available in microfiche. If your local library does not have the relevant issue of a journal, you may be able to obtain a reprint from University Microfilms International (UMI), 300 North Zeeb Road, Ann Arbor, MI 48106. All orders must be accompanied by payment in full, plus postage, and must include the following information: title of the periodical, title of article, name of author, date of issue, volume number, issue number, and page number. Contact UMI for current price information.

Many of the documents in the ERIC system are also available in paper copy from their original publisher. Publisher ordering information is also provided with each entry. Complete publisher ordering information is also listed for all references not in the ERIC system.

<u>Adoption Builds Families Curriculum, Unit I: Family Development</u> and <u>Unit II: Decisions About Self and Family</u> (Social Science Education Consortium, 1980). Available from SSEC Publications, 855 Broadway, Boulder, CO 80302: Unit I--$24.95; Unit II--$32.95.

<u>Family Development</u> is an eight-activity unit that helps elementary students develop understanding of how families are formed, how they change over time, what functions they perform, and what decisions are faced by parents. The kit includes a teacher's guide, two filmstrip/cassettes, posters, and a children's story book. <u>Decisions About Self and Family</u> is a ten-activity unit that helps high school students develop decision-making skills and a clearer understanding of identity through an examination of adoption as a method of building families. The kit contains a teacher's guide, a simulated adoption file, a filmstrip, a cassette program, and a book of student readings. Both kits also include a pamphlet of background information on adoption. "Families in the World of Make-Believe" was developed for this project but does not appear in the published materials.

Barnet, Judith M., "Folk Wit and Wisdom," <u>Intercom 90/91: Culture's Storehouse: Building Humanities Skills Through Folklore</u> (December 1978). EJ 193 325. Reprint available from UMI. <u>Intercom</u> is available from Global Perspectives in Education, 218 East 18th Street, New York, NY 10003: $10.00 per year; $5.00 for issue no. 90/91.

This issue of <u>Intercom</u> was developed as part of GPE's Global Perspectives: A Humanistic Influence on the Curriculum project. The issue contains an article describing that project, along with a rationale for examining folklore around the world. This is followed by seven lessons, many composed of more than one activity, focusing on the study of folklore. All materials needed to use the varied lessons are provided. ERIC/ChESS indexes and annotates selected articles from <u>Intercom</u> for ERIC's <u>Current Index to Journals in Education</u>. <u>Intercom</u> is only one of GPE's many publications in the area of global studies.

Barrett, Junelle and others, <u>Teaching Global Awareness: An Approach for Grades 1-6</u> (Center for Teaching International Relations, University of Denver, 1981). ED 215 923. EDRS price: MF-$0.97. PC available only from CTIR, Dept. S, University of Denver, Denver, CO: $19.95 (includes slides plus $2.00 postage charges).

This book reflects the publisher's view that elementary school is an important place to nurture learning about people who live differently than we do and to develop skills in dealing with other people. The book's 26 activities, which can be used to supplement social studies, reading, language arts, and creative arts classes, are grouped according to four broad objectives for global awareness studies in the elementary grades: "(1) to learn to recognize the interconnection between one's own life, one's society, and major global concerns such as environment, population, resources, and human rights; (2) to develop an understanding of basic human commonalities while recognizing the importance of individual and cultural differences; (3) to develop an awareness of how perceptions, values, and priorities differ among various individuals, groups, and cultures, and (4) to develop the skills that will enable students to respond creatively to local, national, and international events and to participate effectively at those levels."

Bass, Martha and others, TIPS: Crime Resistance Strategies, 6 (Albemarle County and Charlottesville City Schools, 1978). ED 204 229. EDRS price: MF-$0.97. PC available only from TIPS Program, Jefferson Annex, Fourth Street, N.W., Charlottesville, VA 22901: $4.00.

This booklet outlines activities and objectives for a crime prevention education program in the sixth grade. The document is part of a K-8 crime resistance project designed to promote and maintain positive student attitudes and behavior, to assist students in meeting their responsibilities, and to help them ensure their own and other people's safety and welfare. The focus of the sixth-grade component is on teaching students to define such terms as rules, laws, authority, conflict, arbitration, and intervention of authority. A wide variety of activities is suggested.

Building Self Concept: Our Human Ties, Monograph #2 (Los Angeles Unified School District, 1976). ED 212 736. EDRS price: MF-$0.97. PC available only from Los Angeles Unified School District, Instructional Publications Unit, 450 North Grand Avenue, Room G-390, Los Angeles, CA 90012: $16.95 plus 6.5 percent sales tax (for California orders) for set of seven monographs.

This guide presents activities intended to encourage the development of positive attitudes among students and to foster understanding of the interrelatedness among culturally different people as well as the uniqueness of individuals. Forty-four activities are included.

Butzin, Sarah M., "Learning Experiences to Promote Sex Equity," Social Education 45, no. 1 (January 1982), pp. 48-53. EJ 255 689. Reprint available from UMI. Social Education is available from the National Council for the Social Studies, 3501 Newark Street, N.W., Washington, DC 20016: $35.00 per year without membership in NCSS; back issues $5.00.

This article presents five activities that elementary teachers can use to promote awareness of issues related to sex equity. In addition to the "In-Sight Game," the author presents a magazine/newspaper scavenger hunt for items related to sex equity, a textbook scavenger hunt, a role play/guessing game, and an activity in which students invent new words to replace gender-based words. All articles in Social Education are indexed and abstracted by ERIC/ChESS for CIJE.

Criscuolo, Nicholas P., "More Miracle Motivators for Reluctant Readers," Instructor 89, no. 8 (March 1980). Instructor is available from Instructor Publications, Box 6099, Duluth, MN 55806: $18.00 per year; back issues are not generally available.

This article briefly describes a number of reading activities for elementary students. Articles in Instructor (now Instructor and Teacher) are indexed and abstracted for CIJE on a selective basis by the ERIC Clearinghouse on Teacher Education. Reprints of articles indexed in CIJE are available from UMI.

D'Amico, Joseph J. and others, Words Into Action: A Classroom Guide to Children's Citizenship Education (Research for Better Schools, 1980). ED 184 915. EDRS price: MF-$0.97/PC-$7.40. PC also available from Publications Office (Attn: M. Palladino), Research for Better Schools, Inc., 444 North Third Street, Philadelphia, PA 19123: $3.00 (prepayment preferred).

This booklet presents information to help teachers understand three influences on children's citizenship development: role models, institutional environments, and individual development. The book also offers practical suggestions to enrich students' citizenship education experiences. Summarized are citizenship activities for children to do at home or in the community; these are detailed in a related document.

Donaldson, O. Fred, Children are Geographers: Explorations in Space, Instructional Activities Series IA/E-12 (National Council for Geographic Education, 1975). ED 124 456. EDRS price: MF-$0.97. PC available only from NCGE, Western Illinois University, Macomb, IL 61455: $0.60.

This unit, one in a set of teacher-developed materials for elementary geography, emphasizes that children act as geographers in activities that use a classroom as the environment. Exploration and discovery through games and maps are the techniques used for instruction. The first part of the unit provides examples of the geographic perspectives of young people, and the second part suggests three exploration games that can be used to develop geographic awareness.

Forkner, Jerry and Gail Schatz, Consumer Education Learning Activities (Social Science Education Consortium and ERIC Clearinghouse for Social Studies/Social Science Education, 1980). ED 195 486. EDRS price: MF-$0.97/PC-$9.15. PC also available from SSEC Publications, 855 Broadway, Boulder, CO 80302: $10.95.

This handbook contains 24 model lessons on consumer education for use with intermediate, junior high, and high school students. The learning activities are self-contained and can be used in social studies, business, home economics, language arts, math, and science courses. The lessons are divided into nine categories: basic economics of the marketplace; legal rights, redress, and consumer law; financial management and credit; energy consumption and conservation; major purchases; special problems (e.g., advertising, public safety); federal assistance and services; consumer representation; and government regulatory processes. Black-line masters for student handouts are provided.

Giampaolo, Cloe, "A Tasty Time Line," in "Basic Curriculum," Teacher 97, no. 5 (February 1980). Back issues of Teacher are not available.

"Basic Curriculum" was a regular feature of Teacher magazine, which is now incorporated into Instructor. "Basic Curriculum" contained teaching ideas for all areas of the curriculum. For example, the issue that contained "A Tasty Time Line" also included activities entitled "Musical Math," "Basic Skills Bingo," "Twelve Days with Twigs," and

"Unlocking Words Through Syllabication." Selected articles from Teacher were indexed in CIJE. Reprints are available from UMI.

Haley, Francis, ed., Ethnic Studies Sampler: The Best of the Title IX Project Materials (Social Science Education Consortium and ERIC Clearinghouse for Social Studies/Social Science Education, 1981). ED 198 065. EDRS price: MF-$0.97/PC-$30.15. PC also available from SSEC Publications, 855 Broadway, Boulder, CO 80302: $20.00.

This sampler contains selected lessons, activities, and materials produced by ethnic studies projects funded under Title IX of the Elementary and Secondary Education Act. Materials, selected to be useful to a variety of audiences (classroom teachers, university professors, teacher educators, and community groups), are divided into three sections: classroom activities, assessment and design materials, and teacher-training materials. "What Would You Pack?" was developed by the Minneapolis Multi-Ethnic Curriculum Project, whose materials are available through the ERIC system; materials produced by many of the projects represented in the sampler are available through ERIC.

"Handle Holiday Havoc: Teach With Toys!," Keeping Up (December 1982). Keeping Up is available from the ERIC Clearinghouse for Social Studies/Social Science Education, 855 Broadway, Boulder, CO 80302: subscriptions free; back issues free while supply lasts.

This article presents eight ideas for teaching social studies concepts and skills using toys as instructional tools. It appeared in the newsletter of the ERIC Clearinghouse for Social Studies/Social Science Education, which contains information on the ERIC system, the activities of the clearinghouse, and the social studies field in general.

Hawley, Robert and Isabel, Developing Human Potential: A Handbook of Activities for Personal and Social Growth (Education Research Associates, 1975). Available from Education Research Associates, Box 767-EC, Amherst, MA 01004: $8.45 postpaid.

This handbook is designed to help students grow toward "maturity, self-realization, and active social melioration." Its 82 activities can be used by teachers or other youth leaders. They focus on such areas as motivation, self-awareness, communication skills, interpersonal relationships, and creativity. Also covered are methods for teaching standard academic subjects through personal growth activities and evaluation.

Johnson, Jacquelyn and John Benegar, Global Issues in the Intermediate Classroom: Grades 5-8 (Social Science Education Consortium and ERIC Clearinghouse for Social Studies/Social Science Education, 1981). ED 209 125. EDRS price: MF-$0.97/PC-$10.90. PC also available from SSEC Publications, 855 Broadway, Boulder, CO 80302: $8.95.

This publication contains teacher-developed activities for teaching about global issues in grades 5-8. The self-contained activities are organized into three major parts. The first, "Global Awareness," introduces students to the concept of global education. Through the activities in the second part, "Global Interdependence," students learn that they are connected to other people and countries in countless ways and that these links exist across cultures as well as across time and space. The final part of the book contains activities designed to teach cross-cultural understanding. Related resources in the ERIC system are cited.

Klenzman, Elizabeth and Paula Taylor, Creating Futures Activity Cards and Teacher Guide (Minneapolis Public Schools, 1979). ED 201 561. EDRS price: MF-$0.97. PC available only from Federal Programs Dept., Minneapolis Public Schools, 807 Northeast Broadway, Minneapolis, MN 55413: $9.75 plus $2.00 billing charge if payment does not accompany order.

This guide presents learning activities that can be used to teach about the future in elementary and secondary social studies, science, math, language arts, and arts courses. The activities are designed to help students practice creative-thinking skills, investigate problems relevant to their personal futures, experience the concept of change, and evaluate alternatives and make decisions. The activities are presented on cards intended for student use. A teacher's guide accompanies the cards, which are color coded by topic.

Larkin, Robert P. and Paul K. Grogger, Map and Compass Skills for the Elementary School, Instructional Activities Series IA/E-9 (National Council for Geographic Education, 1975). ED 138 529. EDRS price: MF-$0.97. PC available only from NCGE, Western Illinois University, Macomb, IL 61455: $1.75.

This paper describes 20 activities that can be used to develop map and compass skills in elementary grades. The activities range from simple beginners' projects to more complex tasks. Most can be carried out in the classroom, schoolyard, or local neighborhood. Sample diagrams and maps accompany many of the suggested activities.

Mahood, Wayne, "The Land of Milk and Honey," in "Classroom Teacher's 'Idea' Notebook," Social Education 44, no. 1 (January 1980), pp. 22-24. EJ 215 080. Reprint available from UMI. Social Education is available from the National Council for the Social Studies, 3501 Newark Street, N.W., Washington, DC 20016: $35.00 per year without membership in NCSS; back issues $5.00.

"The Land of Milk and Honey," was one of three simulation games presented in this issue of "Classroom Teacher's 'Idea' Notebook," a collection of teaching ideas that appears periodically in Social Education. Other simulations presented were "ECO-TAX: A Simulation Game in Economics" and "Public School Support: Simulating Yesterday, Today, Tomorrow." All articles in Social Education are indexed and abstracted by ERIC/ChESS for CIJE.

Martorella, Peter H. and Jack Madden, No Place to Play: Valuing Dilemmas in the Choice of Recreational Sites, Instructional Activities Series IA/E-7 (National Council for Geographic Education, 1975). ED 124 452. EDRS price: MF-$0.97. PC available only from NCGE, Western Illinois University, Macomb, IL 61455: $0.60.

In this activity, students investigate the selection of recreational sites in urban areas. It is suggested that after completing the case study of Urbo, students examine land use issues in their own community.

Mitchell, Maxine R. and others, Interdependence and Social Interaction: Our Human Ties, Monograph #4 (Los Angeles Unified School District, 1976). ED 212 738. EDRS price: MF-$0.97. PC available only from Los Angeles Unified School District, Instructional Publications Unit, 450 North Grand Avenue, Room G-390, Los Angeles, CA 90012: $16.95 plus 6.5 percent sales tax (for California orders) for set of seven monographs.

Interdependence and social interaction are the topics of this teaching guide. Presented are instructional objectives and activities that promote cross-cultural communication and cooperation in the development of social value systems. Aspects of verbal and nonverbal communication are explored in relation to individual and group behavior. Attitudes toward physical disabilities, color differences, religion, and the environment are also addressed.

Mitsakos, Charles L., Kindergarten Social Studies Program: Teacher's Resource Guide (Chelmsford Public Schools, 1976). ED 153 887. EDRS price: MF-$0.97/PC-$5.65.

This guide presents five units designed to assist kindergarten teachers in developing and implementing social studies programs that introduce children to the world, its resources, and its peoples. Included in the units are resources and activities that correlate basic map and locational skills with global awareness objectives.

Naylor, David T., Learning About Law: A Law-Related Instructional Unit for Children in Grades 5 and 6 (Ohio State Bar Association, 1980). ED 200 501. EDRS price: MF-$0.97/PC-$5.65. PC also available from Ohio State Bar Association, 33 West 11th Avenue, Columbus, OH 43230: $1.00 (three related units are also available for a price of $1.00 each).

This document contains an instructional booklet for teachers and a book of handouts for use by students in fifth- and sixth-grade social studies programs on law-related education. The general objective of the unit is to help elementary school students understand and deal successfully with a variety of rules, responsibilities, and laws. The unit is presented in 14 lessons that involve students in a range of activities.

Nesbitt, William A., "Grab the Bananas: A Simple Example of a Simulation Game," Intercom 75: Teaching Global Issues Through Simulations: It Can Be Easy (Summer 1974). Intercom is available from Global Perspectives in Education, 218 East 18th Street, New York, NY 10003: $10.00 for annual subscription; $1.50 for issue no. 75.

This issue of Intercom provides a guide for the use of simulation games in global education. Along with "Grab the Bananas," the issue provides an adaptation of "The Road Game" and analyzes a number of relevant games, many of which are still available. ERIC/ChESS indexes and annotates selected articles from Intercom for CIJE.

Nesbitt, William A. and others, Teaching Youth About Conflict and War. Teaching Social Studies in an Age of Crisis, Number 5 (National Council for the Social Studies, 1973). ED 079 209. EDRS price: MF-$0.97; PC not available.

This interdisciplinary guide for social studies teachers offers an introductory, objective approach toward the study of conflict and war. The book's basic assumption is that the institution of war is a problem to be studied and is amenable to human intervention and resolution. Teachers are encouraged to employ inquiry and discussion techniques that force youth to raise and analyze values and issues dealing with conflict.

Nethery, Mary and others, The Cultural Exchange: A Cross-Cultural and Interdisciplinary Multicultural Education Curriculum for Grades 4-8 (Humboldt County Office of Education, 1980). ED 202 781. EDRS price: MF-$0.97. PC available only from Humboldt County Office of Education, 901 Myrtle Avenue, Eureka, CA 99501: $60.00 for five books and filmstrip/cassette.

This document provides a variety of values-oriented activities to help students explore, understand, and appreciate culturally diverse values. Activities are matched to one of seven objectives and are cross-referenced to the subject areas of social science, mathematics, fine arts, drama, physical education, language arts, and reading. The seven objectives are for students to (1) identify important elements in a given situation dealing with likenesses and differences among people, (2) act upon chosen values in role playing, (3) define and list different values that people may have in a given situation, (4) define respect, (5) identify prejudice, (6) identify personal dislikes as opposed to prejudice, and (7) demonstrate procedures for coping with values conflict.

Pasternak, Michael G., Helping Kids Learn Multi-Cultural Concepts: A Handbook of Strategies (Research Press, 1979). Available from Research Press, 2612 North Mattis Avenue, Champaign, IL 61820: $9.95 each for 1-9 copies; $8.95 each for 10 or more copies.

Teachers developed the 98 diverse classroom activities presented in this book for use with students aged 10-13, but the activities can be adapted for older or younger students as well. The activities are designed to meet three objectives: "(1) enhancing multi-ethnic and multi-cultural understandings, (2) building healthy human relationships and self-concepts, and (3) improving the multi-cultural climate factors of a school." The book also provides sections on identifying multicultural resources and on leading, organizing, and implementing inservice training for multicultural education.

Pelow, Randall A., <u>Motivational Use of Adaptable Designs in Reinforcing Geographic-Social Studies Content</u>, paper presented at the annual meeting of the National Council for Geographic Education, 1981. ED 214 816. EDRS price: MF-$0.97/PC-$2.15. PC also available from Dr. Randall A. Pelow, Professor of Elementary Education, Shippensburg State College, Shippensburg, PA 17259.

This paper provides teachers with four adaptable designs that can be used to reinforce geographic and social studies knowledge. Adaptable designs are defined as structural formats that can be used repeatedly to teach different concepts and skills. Each design contains a sample section showing how content materials can be applied to it. Several of the activities are presented in game-like formats.

<u>Role of Law in a Free Society and the Rights and Responsibilities of Citizenship, The: A Curriculum Guide for Kindergarten Through Grade 12</u>, revised edition (Missouri State Bar Association and Missouri State Department of Elementary and Secondary Education, 1976). ED 142 450. EDRS price: MF-$0.97/PC-$28.40. PC of 1981 edition also available from the Missouri Bar, ATTN: Field Director, Box 119, Jefferson City, MO 65102: $7.50 in Missouri/$10.00 outside Missouri.

This curriculum guide contains learning objectives, activities, and resources and reinforcement materials to help elementary and secondary teachers develop a legal education unit. Nine major topics are covered: reasons for law, development of the law, functions of the law, the court system, major Supreme Court decisions and their impact on U.S. history, juvenile court, due process, the Bill of Rights in criminal cases, and Bill of Rights protections of civil liberties. More than 200 activities are described in the guide.

Singleton, Laurel R., <u>Social Studies for the Visually Impaired Child</u> (Social Science Education Consortium, 1980). ED 195 466. EDRS price: MF-$0.97. PC available only from SSEC Publications, 855 Broadway, Boulder, CO 80302: $15.00 for set of six sourcebooks.

One of the <u>Project MAVIS Sourcebook Series</u>, this booklet provides suggestions for teaching visually impaired children in the mainstreamed social studies classroom. Topics covered are learning through sensory experiences, learning through discussions, learning through pictures and other illustrations, learning through group activities, and learning through out-of-classroom experiences. Also discussed is working with the resource teacher. Guidelines for adapting social studies materials are presented.

Skeel, Dorothy J. and Ronald Sterling, <u>There's More than the Three R's to Those Early Years</u>, paper presented at the annual meeting of the National Council for the Social Studies, November 1978. ED 162 938. EDRS price: MF-$0.97; PC not available.

This paper presents 12 learning activities to help children in grades K-3 develop skills of valuing, decision making, interpersonal relationships, and spatial awareness. For each of the three activities at each grade level, the paper outlines concepts, objectives, materials, needs, procedures, and evaluation methods.

Smith, Melinda R., ed., <u>Law in U.S. History: A Teacher Resource Manual</u> (New Mexico Law-Related Education Project, 1981). In New Mexico, contact the New Mexico Law-Related Education Project, Box 25883, Albuquerque, NM 87125; not currently available for national distribution. To be published in 1983 by Social Science Education Consortium and ERIC Clearinghouse for Social Studies/Social Science Education. Contact Publications Department, SSEC, 855 Broadway, Boulder, CO 80302 for more information.

This guide contains 37 activities that focus on law-related issues and themes in U.S. history. The activities are grouped into four sections roughly corresponding to the chronological periods covered in most U.S. history courses. The activities employ a variety of instructional strategies and are completely self-contained; all necessary handouts are provided.

Smyka, Kristin, "Exploring the Past: Writing About Real Stuff," in <u>Writing in Elementary School Social Studies</u>, edited by Barry K. Beyer and Robert Gilstrap (Social Science Education Consortium and ERIC Clearinghouse for Social Studies/Social Science Education, 1982), pp. 71-76. ED 213 631. EDRS price: MF-$0.97/PC-$16.15. PC also available from SSEC Publications, 855 Broadway, Boulder, CO 80302: $10.95.

This article is one of 20 in a collection that focuses on practical, classroom-tested techniques that integrate writing and social studies in the elementary grades. Written by experienced teachers, teacher trainers, educational researchers, principals, and curriculum specialists from across the nation, the articles are organized into four sections: "Research on the Teaching of Writing," "Developing Readiness for Writing," "Using Writing to Learn Social Studies Content," and "Combining Writing with Social Studies."

<u>Teacher's Guide for the Basic Competencies in Reasoning</u> (Vermont State Department of Education, 1978). ED 170 190. EDRS price: MF-$0.97/PC-$3.90. PC also available from Vermont State Department of Education, Montpelier, VT 05602: single copies free.

This guide defines the basic competencies in reasoning and describes how to incorporate them into the curriculum at all grade levels. Reasoning is defined as the ability to approach day-to-day problems with intelligent decision-making skills. The four competencies emphasized are problem solving, classifying and organizing, judging, and researching. For each competency, the guide presents sample teaching strategies and mastery-level activities at primary, middle, and upper-grade levels.

Winston, Barbara J. and Charlotte C. Anderson, Skill Development in Elementary Social Studies: A New Perspective (Social Science Education Consortium and ERIC Clearinghouse for Social Studies/Social Science Education, 1977). ED 175 735. EDRS price: MF-$0.97/PC-$6.40. PC also available from SSEC Publications, 855 Broadway, Boulder, CO 80302: $5.95.

This handbook defines skills critical to elementary school students in acquiring and processing information related to social studies. Three broad categories of skills are dealt with: (1) information-acquisition skills (direct observation, using questions, using prepared sources), (2) information-processing skills (comparing, conceptualizing, hypothesizing), and (3) self-management skills (decreasing stereotypic, egocentric, and ethnocentric perceptions). The handbook also suggests teaching strategies for use by elementary teachers as they develop social studies and/or citizenship education programs.